Contents

I.

WHY READ A FINANCIAL STATEMENT?

You got to know when to hold 'em,
Know when to fold 'em ...
– The Gambler (D. Schlitz)

A financial statement quantifies an enterprise's activities and resources in units of currency. The four standard statements are the balance sheet, the income statement, the statement of cash flows, and the statement of owners' equity. Enterprises prepare financial statements at regular intervals, typically quarterly, to furnish managers, owners, creditors, and other interested parties with timely feedback about the results of their activities. In short, financial statements help to distinguish the winners from the losers.

With some analysis, a set of financial statements allows the reader to determine an enterprise's solvency and, if it is a business (rather than a nonprofit organization), its profitability. These determinations are crucial for the smooth functioning of the market economy, because they allow investors, lenders, entrepreneurs, and employees to direct their talents and financial resources toward the most rewarding opportunities, and away from the losers. The ongoing redirection of resources rewards successful managers, prompts poor performers to mend their ways, and minimizes the damage caused by the incompetents. Whenever this feedback is impeded, profitable opportunities go unexploited for lack of financing, and small errors of judgment compound into expensive debacles. Financial statements therefore are important decision-making tools.

Financial statements are products of the accounting process, which begins with simple bookkeeping, the maintenance of records of cash receipts and outlays. Bookkeeping records, such as the "trial balance," are seldom sufficient to provide useful information. Accounting involves the classification of an enterprise's transactions by management to produce financial statements. As such, its effectiveness depends on the rules that guide the accounting process, which vary from country to country. Where the rules are lax, enterprises can retain the confidence of investors and creditors while obscuring profitability and solvency problems. Lax rules also allow businesses to satisfy the tax authorities while obscuring unusual profitability. By forcing enterprises to acknowledge problems promptly, strict rules ensure that accounting produces accountability.

This book covers financial statements prepared under generally accepted accounting principles (GAAP), the set of rules that govern accounting practices in the United States. Much like the common law, GAAP is an evolutionary set of rules that is heavily influenced by practical consider- ations. Since 1917, several professional and regulatory bodies have con- tributed to the codification of GAAP, although much of it is not codified outside of accounting textbooks. Since 1973, the Financial Accounting Standards Board (FASB) has been the principal arbiter of GAAP, although the Securities and Exchange Commission (SEC), the American Institute of Certified Public Accountants (AICPA), and other organizations make ma- jor contributions to its continuing evolution.

Like any product of evolution, GAAP has few aspects that are settled, and many warts and blemishes. Its principles afford accountants consider- able discretion, and accounting practice is a battleground for the compet- ing interests of managers, investors, regulators, auditors, and others. Gen- erally *contested* accounting principles might be a more accurate label, given the current state of affairs. As Abraham Briloff, an eminent authority on less than forthright disclosure, noted recently, "The FASB is constantly playing catch-up with respect to problems that may be festering. And, eventually, possibly clarifying the problems of yesteryear. While it's obvi- ous, largely, to new ones coming along the pike."*

GAAP clearly has its critics, but it is one of the world's strictest bodies of accounting rules. Financial statements produced in the United Kingdom and its former colonies, including the United States, generally are more reliable than those produced elsewhere, but there are several non-English- speaking countries where the reliability of financial disclosures approaches that of GAAP disclosures. At the other end of the spectrum, German and Swiss accounting rules are notoriously permissive, allowing for instant write-offs of brand-new assets, and for reserve funds that pad expenses during good times and profits during bad times. Similar practices prevail in most countries.

The Auditors' Report

In countries that do have strict accounting rules, readers of financial statements still have no assurance that a set of statements complies with those rules unless independent public accountants have audited it. In an American audit, the independent accountants examine an enterprise's accounting records and procedures to determine whether the financial statements conform to GAAP. The auditors themselves must proceed in accordance with generally accepted auditing standards, which require, among other procedures, basic tests of the integrity of an enterprise's books. Auditors advise management of any fraud, embezzlement or the

---

* Welling, Kathryn M., "A Profession's Conscience: Abe Briloff Ponders Accounting's Current State," *Barron's National Business and Financial Weekly* (October 11, 1993), Vol. 73, No. 41, p. 11.

possibilities thereof that are discovered, but contrary to popular belief, this is not their main purpose, which is, to repeat, to certify that the management's accounting is in accordance with GAAP.

By law, financial statements in the annual reports of publicly held corporations must be audited, but the statements of other enterprises are less likely to be audited, and statements in corporate quarterly reports generally are not audited. In the absence of an audit, there is no reasonable assurance that a set of financial statements is reliable. Every set of audited financial statements includes the auditors' report, which notes whether or not the statements are fair presentations that conform to GAAP. **Following the checklist below, readers of financial statements always should turn**

A Checklist

Always remember that financial statements say what managements want to tell you. There is considerable leeway, even within GAAP. Before you begin any of the analyses described in the various chapters of this booklet, we suggest that you first complete the following steps:

1. Read the auditors' report to determine whether or not it is "clean." If the auditors mention items that limit the usefulness of the statements or that violate GAAP, review those items thoroughly.

2. Read the notes to the financial statements, paying particular attention to the organizing principles of the report (this note usually appears first), so that you understand what is and is not included.

3. Scan the asset side of the balance sheet to see if there are any intangibles listed, such as goodwill. The economic value of such assets may be questionable. Also on the asset side, check to see if marketable items, such as inventories and securities, are carried at their current market values. If, instead, they are shown at cost, make appropriate adjustments if their market values are disclosed elsewhere.

4. Scan the liabilities for unusual items. Pay particular attention to the structure of long-term debt, including the current portion, and to commitments and contingencies, if any. Fund balances or equity may have to be adjusted to reflect any questionable asset values found in step 3. Also, for nonprofits, note the extent to which fund balances are restricted, and why.

5. Review the cash flow statement. The additions to, and especially the deductions from, operating cash flows from noncash items can provide valuable clues to unusual accounting practices requiring further scrutiny. Investing and financing activities may reflect important events that are not immediately evident on the balance sheet and income statement.

to the auditors' report first, before proceeding to the financial statements themselves.

Because "clean" opinions, indicating that the auditors have found that the management's statements conform to GAAP, are valuable in relationships with investors and creditors, most managements will accept adjustments suggested by auditors. By the same token, because auditors usually are hired, and fired, by management, auditors usually will accept management's figures unless they fall outside the latitude permitted by GAAP. Accordingly, **readers of financial statements should pay close attention to any qualifications and explanations included in the auditor's opinion** — they can serve as a guide to significant problems that management may be attempting to minimize, or even to portray favorably.

The FASB has set forth highly specific guidelines governing the contents of auditors' reports. As a result, all reports that affirm the reliability of financial statements consist of the same boilerplate language.* The standard report, as shown at right, contains an introductory paragraph, a scope paragraph, and an opinion paragraph. If the auditors' report contains just these three paragraphs, and if the opinion paragraph is unqualified, then the reader can proceed to the financial statements themselves with a reasonable assurance that the statements are reliable. An unqualified opinion affirms that the financial statements are fair presentations in all material respects and that they conform to GAAP. Readers of financial statements should understand clearly the difference between reasonable assurance and absolute assurance. There are many cases of auditors being defrauded, but it takes a substantial effort to obtain an unqualified opinion on books that have been "cooked."

If the opinion paragraph contains language that differs from the example at right, the opinion is qualified. Qualified opinions usually indicate serious doubts about the reliability of the financial statements. Problems with the audited enterprise's accounting practices and limitations in the scope of the audit both can give rise to qualifications. Particularly serious forms of qualification include disclaimers, in which the auditors lack sufficient evidence to express an opinion on the financial statements, and adverse opinions, which indicate material departures from GAAP.

An explanatory paragraph detailing the reasons for qualification usually follows a qualified opinion, but explanatory paragraphs do not always indicate qualifications. The examples in this chapter are cases in point: each of the opinions is "clean," but both include an explanatory paragraph.

---

* For a comprehensive guide to the auditors' report see *Understanding Audits and the Auditors' Report* (New York: American Institute of Certified Public Accountants, 1989).

4

Report of Independent Public Accountants

To the Shareholders of International Paper Company:

We have audited the accompanying consolidated balance sheets of International Paper Company (a New York corporation) and subsidiaries as of December 31, 1992 and 1991, and the related consolidated statements of earnings, common shareholders' equity and cash flows for each of the three years in the period ended December 31, 1992. These financial statements are the responsibility of the Company's management. Our responsibility is to express an opinion on these financial statements based on our audits.

introductory paragraph

We conducted our audits in accordance with generally accepted auditing standards. Those standards require that we plan and perform the audit to obtain reasonable assurance about whether the financial statements are free of material misstatement. An audit includes examining, on a test basis, evidence supporting the amounts and disclosures in the financial statements. An audit also includes assessing the accounting principles used and significant estimates made by management, as well as evaluating the overall financial statement presentation. We believe that our audits provide a reasonable basis for our opinion.

unqualified standard auditors' report

scope paragraph

In our opinion, the financial statements referred to above present fairly, in all material respects, the financial position of International Paper Company and subsidiaries as of December 31, 1992 and 1991, and the results of their operations and their cash flows for each of the three years in the period ended December 31, 1992 in conformity with generally accepted accounting principles.

opinion paragraph

As explained in Notes 5 and 11 to the financial statements, effective January 1, 1992, the Company changed its method of accounting for income taxes, and effective January 1, 1991 changed its method of accounting for postretirement health care and life insurance benefits.

nonstandard explanatory paragraph

[Arthur Andersen & Co.]

New York, N.Y.
February 5, 1993

Adapted from *International Paper Annual Report for 1992* (Purchase, NY: International Paper Company, 1993), p. 41.

Report of Independent Accountants

Price Waterhouse
153 East 53rd Street
New York, New York

To the Board of Directors
and Shareholders
of Woolworth Corporation

*unqualified
Price Waterhouse
report*

In our opinion, the financial statements appearing on pages 22 through 36 of this report present fairly, in all material respects, the financial position of Woolworth Corporation and its consolidated subsidiaries at January 30, 1993, January 25, 1992, and January 26, 1991, and the results of their operations and their cash flows for the years then ended, in conformity with generally accepted accounting principles. These financial statements are the responsibility of the Company's management; our responsibility is to express an opinion on these financial statements based on our audits. We conducted our audits of these statements in accordance with generally accepted auditing standards which require that we plan and perform the audit to obtain reasonable assurance about whether the financial statements are free of material misstatement. An audit includes examining, on a test basis, evidence supporting the amounts and disclosures in the financial statements, assessing the accounting principles used and significant estimates made by management, and evaluating the overall financial statement presentation. We believe that our audits provide a reasonable basis for the opinion expressed above.

*nonstandard
explanatory
paragraph*

As discussed on page 29, in 1991 the Company changed its method of determining retail price indices used in the valuation of certain LIFO inventories. Also in 1991, as discussed on page 34, the Company adopted Statement of Financial Accounting Standards No. 106, "Employers' Accounting for Postretirement Benefits Other Than Pensions."

[Price Waterhouse]

Price Waterhouse
March 2, 1993

Adapted from *Pursuing Strategic Diversification: Annual Report* (New York: Woolworth Corporation, 1993), p. 26.

The most common reasons for adding an explanatory paragraph to an unqualified opinion include changes in accounting principles, as in the examples, and changes in auditors. These changes are important, but they are not likely to affect the reliability of financial statements. The reader should be sure to ascertain the identity and reputation of the previous auditors (the auditors' report does not disclose these facts), and to determine the size of the cumulative effects of changes in accounting principles, which appear in the income statement.

Less common reasons for explanatory paragraphs include material uncertainties, going-concern problems, and matters of emphasis. Of these, matters of emphasis are least likely to affect the reliability of financial statements. Auditors often choose to emphasize an enterprise's dealings at less than arm's length, with officers and their relatives, for example. Material uncertainties are matters that could have a significant future impact on the financial statements, such as pending lawsuits, but which remain unresolved. Going-concern problems arise when an enterprise is perilously close to bankruptcy or insolvency, which can have a major impact on an enterprise's balance sheet. Material uncertainties and going-concern problems are red flags, and are likely to affect the reliability of otherwise fairly presented financial statements. The reader should examine closely the disclosures of these matters in the notes to the financial statements.

Price Waterhouse, one of the "big six" auditing firms, uses a variation on the standard auditors' report. This variation combines the three standard paragraphs into one, as shown at left. The contents of the single paragraph are essentially the same as the contents of the standard report. Nonstandard explanatory items appear in a separate paragraph, which would be the fourth paragraph in the standard format.

INTERNATIONAL PAPER COMPANY

Consolidated Balance Sheet
December 31, 1992

Assets

Current Assets:	(in millions)
Cash and temporary investments, at cost, which approximates market	$ 225
Accounts and notes receivable, less allowance of $91	1,861
Inventories	1,938
Other current assets	342
Total Current Assets	$ 4,366
Plants, Properties, and Equipment, net of depreciation	8,884
Forestlands	759
Investments	599
Goodwill	772
Deferred Charges and Other Assets	1,079
Total Assets	**$16,459**

Liabilities and Common Shareholders' Equity

Current Liabilities:	
Notes payable and current maturities of long-term debt	$ 2,356
Accounts payable	1,259
Accrued payroll and benefits	173
Accrued income taxes	104
Other accrued liabilities	639
Total Current Liabilities	$ 4,531
Long-Term Debt	3,096
Deferred Income Taxes	1,417
Minority Interest and Other Liabilities	1,226
Commitments and contingent liabilities	
Total Liabilities	$10,270
Common Shareholders' Equity:	
Common stock, $1 par value (127.0 shares issued)	$ 127
Paid-in capital	1,792
Retained earnings	4,472
Common stock held in treasury, at cost (4.3 shares)	(202)
Total Common Shareholders' Equity	$ 6,189
Total Liabilities and Common Shareholders' Equity	**$16,459**

Adapted from *International Paper Annual Report for 1992* (Purchase, NY: International Paper Company, 1993), p. 43. The notes on pp. 46-52 of the *Annual Report* are an integral part of the original statement.

II.

THE BALANCE SHEET

A balance sheet provides a snapshot of an enterprise's financial position on a given date. It lists the values of the enterprise's assets, liabilities, and equity on that date, usually the end of an accounting period. In the United States, a balance sheet customarily lists assets first, followed by liabilities and then equity (for businesses) or net assets (for nonprofit organizations). As the example at left shows, a balance sheet is a highly condensed enumeration of an enterprise's accounts. The published balance sheet of a large corporation compresses the balances of thousands of individual accounts into roughly 30 numbers. Synonyms for balance sheet include statement of financial condition, statement of condition, statement of financial position, and statement of assets and liabilities.

By law, balance sheets that appear in the annual reports of publicly traded corporations must be comparative balance sheets, which show the values of each line item at the end of two comparable accounting periods. Many enterprises not subject to this law also provide comparative balance sheets. The example at left is adapted from an annual report, but for the sake of simplicity it reports values for only one date.

The example follows the customary practice among businesses of presenting financial statements on a consolidated basis, which means that the accountants have added together the positions of all of the enterprise's subsidiaries and divisions to produce a total for the whole enterprise for each line item. The usual practice among nonprofit enterprises is to report the positions of various funds, which segregate the assets, liabilities, and net assets attributable to the major activities of the organization. Many nonprofits also report consolidated totals.

The balance sheet is so named because it balances an enterprise's assets against the two categories of claims on those assets, liabilities and equity (net assets). All balance sheets balance because equity (net assets) is a residual — by definition it is the difference between assets and liabilities:

(1) $$\text{equity} = \text{assets} - \text{liabilities}$$

Legally, the owners of a business hold an equity interest, a claim to that portion of assets left over after the business has settled all claims held by outsiders. The claims held by outsiders are liabilities. A nonprofit organization, which has no owners, holds a claim on its own net assets, which it computes in the same way that a business computes equity:

(2) $$\text{net assets} = \text{assets} - \text{liabilities}$$

9

A rearrangement of Equation (1) gives the fundamental equation of accounting:

(3) $$\text{assets} = \text{liabilities} + \text{equity}$$

This fundamental equation illustrates the balance in the balance sheet. The two sides of the equation represent the two main sections of every balance sheet. "Assets" in the equation corresponds to

Total Assets · **$16,459**

in the example. Similarly, "liabilities + equity" corresponds to

Total Liabilities and Common Shareholders' Equity · · · · · · · · · · · · · · · · · **$16,459**.

As promised, the amounts on both lines are equal.

Assets and Valuation

The economic resources that an enterprise controls are its assets. Such resources can be physical (inventory and equipment, for example), technical (patented designs and processes, software, trademarks), or financial (cash, notes receivable, etc.). The main characteristic of assets is that an enterprise can exchange them for cash or use them to generate cash inflows indirectly. Although such cash flows are prospective, assets themselves are not.

The value of an asset as stated on the balance sheet is its carrying value. In general, a balance sheet carries assets at their cost to the enterprise. The primary advantage of using this "cost principle" of valuation is that cost is easy to determine compared to, say, appraised value, market value (especially when there is no active market in an asset), and replacement cost. There are, however, many exceptions to the cost principle. If an asset has a readily ascertainable market value, for example, the lower of cost or market rule requires an enterprise to carry the asset at market value (less anticipated selling expenses) if that remains lower than the asset's cost for an extended period. Similarly, if an enterprise estimates that loss, damage, theft, spoilage, default, or other mishaps have had a material effect on the value of an asset, the enterprise must write down the carrying value of that asset accordingly:

Accounts and notes receivable, less allowance of $91   1,861

The allowance in this example is an allowance for uncollectible accounts, *i.e.*, the amount of credit granted to customers that is estimated to be at risk of default. International Paper holds outstanding receivables on $1,952 million of sales, of which it estimates it will not collect $91 million, resulting in a net realizable value of receivables of $1,861 million.

Assets that contribute to an enterprise's operations over a useful life of many accounting periods, such as buildings and equipment, require another type of adjustment to historical cost. In order to match properly the revenue generated in each accounting period with the expenses incurred to generate that revenue, enterprises systematically allocate the costs of these types of assets over an estimated useful life. The generic term for this allocation of costs is amortization. The amortization of the cost of buildings and equipment is depreciation, and the amortization of the cost of acquiring natural resources is depletion. The carrying value of an amortizable asset decreases during its estimated useful life as an additional portion of its original cost is allocated to expenses for each passing accounting period. The carrying value of such an asset on any particular date is thus its original cost less the cumulative amortization to date.

Despite the variety of adjustments to historical cost, the asset values that a balance sheet reports often bear only a vague resemblance to replacement costs or market values. One factor that figures significantly in the distortion of balance sheet valuations is the chronic price inflation of the past 6 decades. As prices rise, the carrying values of inventories, equity securities, land, equipment, and other types of assets tend to become increasingly detached from current market conditions. The carrying value of a parcel of land acquired 20 or 30 years ago can differ dramatically from its resale value, for example. Although there are strong practical justifications for an accounting system based on historical costs, users of financial statements should be well aware of the ludicrous valuations that such a system can produce.

Even when cost is indisputably a sound basis for valuation, changing prices still can produce difficulties in valuation. There are no less than four acceptable methods for valuing assets accumulated during a period of changing prices. Inventory valuation is the most common use of these methods. Enterprises that hold inventories disclose the valuation method or methods that they use in the notes to their financial statements.

In the case of retail inventories, the last-in, first-out (LIFO) method attributes the unit prices of lots purchased most recently to sales for the latest period, and uses the unit prices of earlier purchases to value the remaining inventory. The first-in, first-out (FIFO) method takes just the opposite approach, valuing inventory at the unit prices of the most recently purchased lots. The average cost method values inventory at the weighted average unit price of all lots purchased. Given the prevailing upward trend of prices, LIFO produces lower valuations than the average-cost method, which in turn produces lower valuations than FIFO. The fourth valuation method is specific identification, in which the value of an inventory is the sum of the costs of each individual item. This method is the norm for expensive, readily identifiable items such as cars, jewelry, and machinery.

11

Types of Assets

A useful means of understanding the derivation and significance of balance sheet items, one seldom mentioned in the United States, is the British distinction between *personal, real,* and *nominal* accounts. All of the entries on a balance sheet fall in one or another of these classifications. The significance of these categories may not be intuitively obvious from their names, however.

In this framework, personal accounts are simply what the accounting entity owes to or is due from others. Such accounts include bank balances, IOUs of all kinds, accounts payable and receivable, etc. What such items have in common is that their value in terms of currency can be determined with a degree of certainty, as when a depositor, borrower, customer or supplier receives a letter from an auditor requesting "confirmation" of the balance that the auditor has found on the books of the entity he or she is auditing.

Real accounts, on the other hand, reflect an estimate of the value of tangible assets such as inventories, land, buildings, and equipment. This estimate is usually what the accounting entity paid to acquire the asset, which may be markedly different from the economic value of the item on the date of the balance sheet. Real accounts then are real in the sense that they represent real things that the entity owns (you can touch or kick them), but they can be quite "unreal" in terms of what an item might fetch in the marketplace or what it is worth to the entity as a going concern. In the instances of inventories and liquid securities, auditors often attempt to determine current prices and indicate both the cost and the market values on a balance sheet, but this seldom is done for nondepreciable assets such as land or for investments in closely held affiliates, such as joint ventures. Also, the accumulated depreciation on assets such as buildings or equipment may or may not serve to adjust the reported costs of such items to their current values.

Nominal accounts reflect entries that are purely internal to the accounting entity, as when a period's earnings are added to net worth or when the accumulated depreciation is deducted from the cost of real assets. Nominal accounts often are deemed to be the most significant by financial analysts, even though they are completely derivative and least connected to fact.

Another important classification of accounts is the distinction between current and noncurrent items. Current assets include assets that will be converted to cash within 1 year or within the average duration of one operating cycle, whichever is longer, and cash itself. A balance sheet lists

12

current assets in order of decreasing liquidity: cash always tops the list, and the asset listed last is likely to take the most time and effort to convert to cash.

Current Assets:	(in millions)
Cash and temporary investments, at cost, which approximates market	$ 225
Accounts and notes receivable, less allowance of $91	1,861
Inventories	1,938
Other current assets	342
Total Current Assets ·	$ 4,366

These are the assets that an enterprise liquidates regularly. An enterprise does so by direct exchange of noncash assets for cash, or by conversion of noncash assets to other current assets, which the enterprise then exchanges for cash. Examples of direct exchange transactions include the liquidation of receivables, either by their sale to third parties or by the receipt of cash from debtors, and cash sales of finished goods inventories. Indirect liquidations involve sequences of transactions, as in this example: a manufacturer converts materials inventories and supplies into finished goods inventories, which it then exchanges for accounts receivable, which it eventually converts into cash.

In practice, not all current assets appear in the current assets section, and not all assets that appear there are current. International Paper, for example, does not list as a current asset the amount of trees that it expects to harvest, convert to paper, and sell within the next operating cycle. It lumps these trees together with land and noncurrent trees in the forestlands account. Similarly, oil companies do not list any portion of oil in the ground among their current assets. In addition, no enterprise lists as a current asset the portion of fixed assets expected to be used up during the next operating cycle. Noncurrent assets that appear in the current section include notes receivable that mature in more than a year, supplies used to maintain fixed assets, slow-moving and obsolete inventories, and insurance premiums paid more than a year in advance.

Noncurrent assets generate cash flows indirectly, but they do so over the course of many operating cycles. They differ from current assets that generate cash flows indirectly because an enterprise does not use up or liquidate noncurrent assets completely in the course of normal operations. This is not to say that enterprises do not liquidate long-term investments or that equipment does not wear out or become obsolete, but enterprises typically acquire investments and equipment with the intent of holding them for many years. In recognition of these long holding periods, noncurrent assets appear below current assets on the balance sheet,

13

Total Current Assets ·	$ 4,366
Plants, Properties and Equipment, net of depreciation	8,884
Forestlands	759
Investments	599
Goodwill	772
Deferred Charges and Other Assets	1,079
Total Assets ·	**$16,459**

even though some noncurrent assets, notably investments in marketable securities, are as liquid as current assets.

There are two varieties of noncurrent assets: there are the physical and technical assets that an enterprise actively uses to generate cash flows and there are financial assets, investments, that an enterprise holds as a source of passive cash flows. The distinction between these two varieties is not always clear, because enterprises can hold investments in related enterprises in order to ensure smooth operations in their own lines of business. Manufacturers often hold stakes in their parts and raw materials suppliers, for example. Such "synergy" is a common justification for corporate acquisitions. Financial businesses are another example in which the distinction is unclear. Financial businesses actively seek to generate cash flows by making loans to or investments in other businesses.

Accounting for an enterprise's investments in affiliated companies can be complex, especially when the affiliated companies are not subsidiaries. A subsidiary is a company in which the controlling enterprise owns enough of the equity of that company to control the election of the board of directors. Such a controlling interest generally consists of 50 percent or more of the subsidiary's voting stock. In most cases, enterprises consolidate the assets and liabilities of subsidiaries in their published financial statements. Consolidation involves adding all the balances of a subsidiary's accounts to the comparable accounts of the parent and netting out the results of transactions between parent and subsidiary. When an enterprise uses a method other than consolidation, generally when accounting for a minority interest in an affiliate, the enterprise counts its equity interest in the affiliate as an asset:

Investments	599

When an enterprise buys another business outright, it merges the asset and liability accounts of the acquisition with its own, recording the acquisition's accounts at fair market value. This process is different than consolidation because the acquisition does not maintain a separate set of accounting records after the merger — it is not a subsidiary. When the acquiring enterprise pays more than the fair market value of the acquisition's net identifiable assets, it accounts for the excess payment as goodwill. Net

14

identifiable assets are total assets less the sum of total liabilities and previously acquired goodwill. Goodwill represents the acquiring enterprise's recognition of the acquisition's potential for above-average earnings. Similarly, deferred charges reflect outlays that management has decided not to expense immediately because it expects that they will benefit the enterprise for some time to come.

Liabilities

Liabilities are obligations that an enterprise has incurred in past transactions. An enterprise settles liabilities by transferring assets, usually cash, to its obligees or by using its assets to provide services to its obligees. Liabilities are thus claims on an enterprise's assets. There are two important differences between liabilities and equity: first, liabilities are claims held by outsiders, whereas equity is the aggregate claim of a business's owners; second, the amount of an enterprise's liabilities is independent of the amount of its assets, whereas the amount of equity depends on the amounts of assets and liabilities both, as shown in Equation (1).

Priority for settlement is the guiding principle for ordering the items in the bottom half of a balance sheet. Among liabilities, therefore, current items appear first:

Current Liabilities:

Notes payable and current maturities of long-term debt	$ 2,356
Accounts payable	1,259
Accrued payroll and benefits	173
Accrued income taxes	104
Other accrued liabilities	639
Total Current Liabilities	$ 4,531

Much like current assets, current liabilities are those that an enterprise expects to settle within a year or within the average duration of one operating cycle, whichever is longer. Noncurrent liabilities, often called long-term liabilities, are those an enterprise does not expect to settle within this time frame. The placement of noncurrent liabilities reflects this lower priority:

Total Current Liabilities	$ 4,531
Long-Term Debt	3,096
Deferred Income Taxes	1,417
Minority Interest and Other Liabilities	1,226
Commitments and contingent liabilities	
Total Liabilities	$10,270

Most of a typical enterprise's liabilities are obligations to pay cash. These cash obligations fall into two categories: accrued expenses, which

15

an enterprise incurs by purchasing goods and services for which payment is not due immediately, and outstanding debt, which an enterprise incurs by borrowing cash. Most noncash liabilities represent payment in advance for goods or services. By accepting advance payment for goods or services, a business incurs an obligation to provide them. Stadiums, landlords, magazines, and brain surgeons are examples of businesses that incur noncash liabilities for advance payments.

A different type of noncash liability is minority interest in a subsidiary. Minority interest is the share of a subsidiary's net assets that its minority shareholders own. Minority interest differs from other types of liabilities because of its equity characteristics: the bankruptcy liquidation of a subsidiary is the only situation that can force an enterprise to settle its obligation to minority shareholders. The only other circumstances that oblige an enterprise to settle with minority shareholders are those that the enterprise itself initiates, either by buying out some or all of the minority shareholders or by dissolving the subsidiary.

Deferred income taxes are similar to minority interest: technically they are obligations to pay cash, but in practice an enterprise is not likely ever to have to settle the bulk of its deferred tax liabilities. Due to the peculiarities of tax allocation, a subject too complex to explain here, deferred income taxes grow or remain stable under most circumstances. Some balance sheets include an asset called "deferred income taxes," but that item represents prepaid income taxes. Although deferred income tax assets also are a product of tax allocation, they should not be confused with deferred income tax liabilities.

Many enterprises include a line for commitments and contingent liabilities in the liabilities section of the balance sheet. Unlike other line items, this line does not report a dollar value, because commitments and contingencies are not strictly liabilities. The reason for including the line is to alert the reader to further disclosure of these items in the notes to the financial statements. Commitments are agreements, usually formal contracts, to transact business in the future. Examples of commitments include purchase orders, long-term purchase and supply contracts, lines of credit, and employment contracts. Contingent liabilities are losses or obligations that may result from past events or transactions, pending some future outcome or decision. Examples of contingent liabilities include loan guarantees and pending litigation. These items are not liabilities because an enterprise reporting them has yet to experience the transactions or events that would create formal obligations.

Equity

As discussed at the beginning of this chapter, equity is the ownership interest in the assets of a business, defined as the residual assets remaining after all liabilities have been settled:

$$(1) \qquad \text{equity} = \text{assets} - \text{liabilities}$$

A nonprofit enterprise computes its net assets similarly, but net assets do not constitute an ownership interest. In accounting jargon, book value and capital are synonyms for equity and surplus is a synonym for net assets. Net worth is used as a synonym for both equity and net assets.

Increases in the equity of a business come from two sources: income and the contributions of owners. Increases in the net assets of a nonprofit enterprise also come from two sources: income and donations. Similarly, there are two reasons for decreases in the equity of a business: losses and distributions to owners. A nonprofit enterprise has no owners, so its net assets decrease only when it incurs losses.

A business's legal form of organization strongly influences the terms of ownership of its equity, so the line items that appear in the equity section of the business's balance sheet largely reflect the legal form of organization. The balance sheets of small partnerships include a line item for the accumulated equity of each partner:

SMITH, DOE & JONES
Balance Sheet
December 31, 19__
⋮

Partners' Capital:	
J. Smith, capital	$45,000
J. Doe, capital	23,000
T. Jones, capital	15,000
Total Partners' Capital ·	$83,000

⋮

When there are so many partners that this form of presentation becomes cumbersome, the balance sheet may report equity as a single line item. The balance sheets of sole proprietorships also follow this form:

JOHN SMITH, M.D.
Balance Sheet
December 31, 19__
⋮

Total Liabilities ·	$100,000
J. Smith, M.D., Capital	50,000
Total Liabilities and Proprietor's Capital ·	**$150,000**

Partnerships and sole proprietorships that have accumulated substantial

17

losses may show deficits. In these two types of business, a deficit is simply negative equity, which arises when total liabilities exceed total assets:

JOHN SMITH, M.D.
Balance Sheet
December 31, 19__
:

Total Liabilities. ·	$125,000
J. Smith, M.D., Deficit	(10,000)
Total Liabilities and Proprietor's Capital ·	**$115,000**

Returning to our International Paper Company example, it is clear that the stockholders' equity section of a corporate balance sheet generally is more complex than the foregoing examples:

Common Shareholders' Equity:

Common stock, $1 par value (127.0 shares issued)	$ 127
Paid-in capital	1,792
Retained earnings	4,472
Common stock held in treasury, at cost (4.3 shares)	(202)
Total Common Shareholders' Equity	$ 6,189

This example is representative of the standard form of a stockholders' equity section, but the form of the section and the names of the line items vary widely. A few corporations present stockholders' equity as a line item in their published balance sheets, just as a sole proprietor or a large partnership would.

Par value, also called stated value, is a corporation's legal minimum equity position. A corporation's directors cannot declare a dividend (dividends are paid out of equity) that would reduce total equity below the total par value of the corporation's stock. This restriction rarely is a practical consideration, and some states do not require a corporation to establish a par value for its stock. Each class of stock, if there is more than one, has its own per-share par value. The total par value of a class of stock is simply the per-share par value multiplied by the number of shares outstanding:

Common stock, $1 par value (127.0 shares issued)	$ 127

Nearly all stocks sell for much more than par value, so when a corporation issues stock, it accounts for its receipts in excess of par value as paid-in capital, also called additional paid-in capital and capital surplus.

Corporations that have more than one class of stock typically have one or more classes of preferred stock, although some offer several varieties of common stock. Preferred stock is preferred as to dividends, because a corporation cannot pay a dividend on common stock if it is in arrears on its preferred dividends. Preferred stock also takes priority over common stock in liquidation proceedings. Aside from these two distinguishing features, there is a wide variety of other features that corporations use to make preferred stocks attractive to investors. The most common additional feature is a fixed dividend rate, which makes a preferred stock resemble a bond.

Some preferred stocks have a redemption value. Depending on the terms of redemption, the combination of fixed dividend rate and redemption provision may make a redeemable preferred issue indistinguishable from a bond. If the consequences to the corporation of a failure to redeem are sufficiently severe, the preferred issue will appear in the liabilities section of the balance sheet.

To the extent that a corporation does not pay out all of its earnings as dividends, it accumulates retained earnings, a component of equity. The use of retained earnings is a common way for profitable corporations to expand their operations. Corporations that have suffered serious losses may show a deficit, which denotes *negative retained earnings*, not negative equity. Partnerships and sole proprietorships differ from corporations because they do not distinguish between retained earnings and paid-in capital, so a deficit for those types of business is simply negative equity.

The par value of one or more classes of stock, additional paid-in capital, and retained earnings appear in the equity sections of nearly all corporate balance sheets. Many balance sheets also show some adjustments to the total of these core equity items. The three most common adjustments are treasury stock, a deduction related to employee stock ownership plans (ESOPs), and a foreign currency translation adjustment.

Treasury stock is stock that a corporation has issued and subsequently repurchased. The usual reasons for doing so are to administer dividend reinvestment programs and to meet the conversion requests of holders of convertible preferred stock and convertible bonds. Also, some corporations announce stock buy-back programs to bolster investor confidence during stock market declines. Other reasons for share buy-backs include discouraging takeover attempts, preparing to go private, and preparing to acquire other companies.

Corporations distinguish between treasury stock and stock that has been authorized but not yet issued because usually it is much easier to resell treasury stock than it is to issue new shares. Treasury stock appears on the balance sheet as a deduction from equity. Absent other adjustments, total equity is the equity in outstanding shares, which is the sum of the par value of stock, additional paid-in capital, and retained earnings, less any holdings of treasury stock. When a corporation's ESOP purchases stock to distribute to employees, the corporation accounts for the undistributed stock much like treasury stock, but it makes a separate adjustment to equity. Corporations account for treasury stock and ESOP stock separately because the use of ESOP stock is restricted, whereas a corporation can use treasury stock for any purpose.

When an enterprise's financial statements include foreign subsidiaries on a consolidated basis, the parent enterprise must report a cumulative foreign currency translation adjustment in the equity section of the balance sheet. This adjustment is necessary because the arcane accounting rules pertaining to foreign subsidiaries require the parent to translate the equity accounts of the subsidiary at a different exchange rate than that used for the asset and liability accounts. The translation adjustment cumulates the resulting discrepancies over time.

Donations are a major source of increases in the net assets of nonprofit enterprises. It is common for donors to place restrictions on the use of donations. The line items in the net assets section of a nonprofit enterprise's balance sheet reflect the major categories of restrictions:

WESLEYAN UNIVERSITY
Balance Sheet
June 30, 1992

⋮

Fund Balances:	(in thousands)
Government programs — refundable	$ 3,114
University funds:	
Unrestricted	11,633
Restricted	5,113
Endowment	153,156
Quasi-endowment — restricted	5,215
Quasi-endowment — unrestricted	89,534
Life income	8,302
Investment in plant	66,432
Total fund balances	$342,499

⋮

Adapted from *Report of the Treasurer for the Year Ended June 30, 1992* (Middletown, CT: Wesleyan University, 1992), p. 45.

In accounting jargon, fund balances are roughly equivalent to net assets, although the phrase "fund balances" refers to the subtotals for the enterprise's various funds (not shown) as well as to the consolidated total. "Net assets" refers strictly to the consolidated total. Presentation of the net assets section can vary widely from that of the example above, because the particular line items included depend on the activities, especially the fund-raising activities, of the enterprise in question.

III.

ANALYSIS OF THE BALANCE SHEET

A single line item extracted from a financial statement imparts little information. Even a whole financial statement typically contains just 30 numbers, although comparisons among the numbers produce additional quantitative information. A current financial statement becomes more valuable when the reader can compare it to statements from previous accounting periods. The availability of multi-year financial statements for comparable enterprises increases the value of each individual statement even further. In general, the usefulness of a financial statement or any other quantitative information hinges on what one analyst has called "... the question at the heart of quantitative thinking: 'Compared to what?'"*

Analysis of a set of financial statements involves three types of comparisons: the relative sizes of items within a set of statements, the changes in each item and in the relative sizes of items, and the relationships of the key financial measures of an enterprise to those of comparable enterprises or to industry averages. Analysis of the relative sizes of items is called both vertical analysis and ratio analysis. Vertical analysis is the comparison of individual line items in a statement with a single benchmark item, say, sales or total assets. Ratio analysis involves more complex comparisons among various groups of line items, using a variety of benchmarks. Analysis of changes over time in line items and ratios is called horizontal analysis.

The sample analysis of the International Paper balance sheet on the next two pages illustrates the use of horizontal, vertical, and ratio analysis.† Readers who are at ease with computers will find spreadsheet software to be well-suited for preparing this type of analysis. As the note to the sample analysis indicates, it takes two annual reports, each with 2 years of comparative balance sheet data, to prepare a 4-year horizontal analysis. A 3-year analysis is barely adequate for examining the state of an enterprise's finances. The examination of 5 or more years is ideal. When using several reports to prepare a horizontal analysis, the analyst should be alert for restatements of previous years' results to reflect changes in accounting practices.

Vertical analysis requires the analyst to compute common-size statements, which show the proportions of each line item within a statement. A common-size balance sheet expresses each line item as a decimal fraction

---

* Tufte, Edward R., *The Visual Display of Quantitative Information* (Cheshire, CT: Graphics Press, 1983), p. 74.

† Having a photocopy of these two pages at hand will make the rest of this chapter easier to follow.

INTERNATIONAL PAPER COMPANY
Sample Analysis of Balance Sheet

(in millions, except as noted, at December 31)

1989	1990	1991	1992	Assets
$ 102	$ 256	$ 238	$ 225	Cash and Temporary Investments, at cost
1,517	1,798	1,841	1,861	Accounts and Notes Receivable, net
1,355	1,638	1,780	1,938	Inventories
122	247	272	342	Other Current Assets
$ 3,096	$ 3,939	$ 4,131	$ 4,366	*Total Current Assets* · · · · · · · · · · ·
6,238	7,287	7,848	8,884	Plants, Properties, and Equipment, net of depreciation
764	751	743	759	Forestlands
467	103	383	599	Investments
469	687	816	772	Goodwill
548	902	1,020	1,079	Deferred Charges and Other Assets
$11,582	**$13,669**	**$14,941**	**$16,459**	**Total Assets** · · · · · · · · · · ·

Liabilities and Common Shareholders' Equity

1989	1990	1991	1992	
$ 1,017	$ 1,087	$ 1,699	$ 2,356	Notes Payable and Current Maturities of Long-Term Debt
934	1,094	1,110	1,259	Accounts Payable
146	195	216	173	Accrued Payroll and Benefits
145	150	102	104	Accrued Income Taxes
488	629	600	639	Other Accrued Liabilities
$ 2,730	$ 3,155	$ 3,727	$ 4,531	*Total Current Liabilities* · · · · · · · · · ·
2,324	3,096	3,351	3,096	Long-Term Debt
1,020	1,135	1,044	1,417	Deferred Income Taxes
361	651	1,080	1,226	Minority Interest and Other Liabilities
				Commitments and Contingent Liabilities
$ 6,435	$ 8,037	$ 9,202	$10,270	*Total Liabilities* · · · · · · · · · ·
$ 117	$ 117	$ 118	$ 127	Common Stock, $1 par value
1,161	1,243	1,264	1,792	Paid-in Capital
4,195	4,581	4,592	4,472	Retained Earnings
(326)	(309)	(235)	(202)	Common Stock Held in Treasury, at cost
$ 5,147	$ 5,632	$ 5,739	$ 6,189	*Total Common Shareholders' Equity*
$11,582	**$13,669**	**$14,941**	**$16,459**	**Total Liabilities and Common Shareholders' Equity** · · · · · · · ·

Addenda

1989	1990	1991	1992	
$ 366	$ 784	$ 404	$ (165)	Working Capital (current assets less current liabilities)
1,619	2,054	2,079	2,086	Quick Assets (cash, temporary investments, and receivables)
3,705	4,882	5,475	5,739	Long-Term Liabilities (total liabilities less current liabilities)
6,142	5,869	7,956	8,172	Market Value of Equity
116,988	117,303	117,578	126,993	Common Shares Issued (thousands) · · · · · · · · · ·
108,712	109,709	112,454	122,662	Common Shares Outstanding (thousands)
$46.78	$50.65	$50.81	$50.33	Book Value per Common Share Issued
56.500	53.500	70.750	66.625	Market Value per Common Share Outstanding · · · · · · · · · · ·
1.13	1.25	1.11	0.96	Current Ratio
0.59	0.65	0.56	0.46	Quick Assets Ratio
0.56	0.59	0.62	0.62	Debt Ratio
1.25	1.43	1.60	1.66	Debt-Equity Ratio
0.42	0.46	0.49	0.48	Capitalization Ratio
0.72	0.87	0.95	0.93	Ratio of Long-Term Liabilities to Equity

Adapted from *International Paper Annual Report for 1990*, p. 48, and *International Paper Annual Report for 1992*, p. 43 (Purchase, NY: International Paper Company, 1991 and 1993). The notes in each *Annual Report* are integral parts of the original statements.

	As fractions of total assets* (common-size statements)			As percentages of 1989 levels (index numbers or trend percentages)			Annual percent changes		
1989	1990	1991	1992	1990	1991	1992	1990	1991	1992
0.01	0.02	0.02	0.01	251%	233%	221%	151.0%	−7.0%	−5.5%
0.13	0.13	0.12	0.11	119	121	123	18.5	2.4	1.1
0.12	0.12	0.12	0.12	121	131	143	20.9	8.7	8.9
0.01	0.02	0.02	0.02	202	223	280	102.5	10.1	25.7
0.27	0.29	0.28	0.27	· · · 127	133	141	· · · · · 27.2	4.9	5.7
0.54	0.53	0.53	0.54	117	126	142	16.8	7.7	13.2
0.07	0.05	0.05	0.05	98	97	99	−1.7	−1.1	2.2
0.04	0.01	0.03	0.04	22	82	128	−77.9	271.8	56.4
0.04	0.05	0.05	0.05	146	174	165	46.5	18.8	−5.4
0.05	0.07	0.07	0.07	165	186	197	64.6	13.1	5.8
1.00	1.00	1.00	1.00	· · · 118	129	142	· · · · · 18.0	9.3	10.2
0.09	0.08	0.11	0.14	107	167	232	6.9	56.3	38.7
0.08	0.08	0.07	0.08	117	119	135	17.1	1.5	13.4
0.01	0.01	0.01	0.01	134	148	118	33.6	10.8	−19.9
0.01	0.01	0.01	0.01	103	70	72	3.4	−32.0	2.0
0.04	0.05	0.04	0.04	129	123	131	28.9	−4.6	6.5
0.24	0.23	0.25	0.28	· · · 116	137	166	· · · · · 15.6	18.1	21.6
0.20	0.23	0.22	0.19	133	144	133	33.2	8.2	−7.6
0.09	0.08	0.07	0.09	111	102	139	11.3	−8.0	35.7
0.03	0.05	0.07	0.07	180	299	340	80.3	65.9	13.5
0.56	0.59	0.62	0.62	· · · 125	143	160	· · · · · 24.9	14.5	11.6
0.01	0.01	0.01	0.01	100	101	109	0.0	0.9	7.6
0.10	0.09	0.08	0.11	107	109	154	7.1	1.7	41.8
0.36	0.34	0.31	0.27	109	109	107	9.2	0.2	−2.6
(0.03)	(0.02)	(0.02)	(0.01)	95	72	62	−5.2	−23.9	−14.0
0.44	0.41	0.38	0.38	109	112	120	9.4	1.9	7.8
1.00	1.00	1.00	1.00	· · · 118	129	142	· · · · · 18.0	9.3	10.2
0.03	0.06	0.03	(0.01)	214	110	(45)			
0.14	0.15	0.14	0.13	127	128	129	26.9	1.2	0.3
0.32	0.36	0.37	0.35	132	148	155	31.8	12.1	4.8
0.53	0.43	0.53	0.50	96	130	133	−4.4	35.6	2.7
				100	101	109	· · · · · · 0.3	0.2	8.0
				101	103	113	0.9	2.5	9.1
				108	109	108	8.3	0.3	−1.0
				95	125	118	· · · · · −5.3	32.2	−5.8

current ratio   = current assets ÷ current liabilities
quick assets ratio   = quick assets ÷ current liabilities
debt ratio   = total liabilities ÷ total assets
debt-equity ratio   = total liabilities ÷ total equity
capitalization ratio   = long-term liabilities ÷ (long-term liabilities + total equity)

* Detail items may not add up to totals because of round-off error.

of total assets. In the sample analysis, the first four columns on the right-hand page illustrate this technique. The example reveals that fixed assets dominate the assets section of International Paper's balance sheet, and that receivables and inventories also are important line items. In the liabilities and common shareholders' equity sections, the most prominent items are long-term debt and retained earnings. Notes payable and current maturities of long-term debt also have become prominent in recent years.

Taken together, forestlands and plants, properties, and equipment account for roughly 60 percent of International Paper's assets. A much lower proportion of fixed assets in the total assets of a manufacturing business would be a cue for the analyst to check the notes to the financial statements for noncancellable operating leases. In theory, operating leases are short-term rentals and capital leases are a way of financing ownership, but in practice the distinction is not always clear. Noncancellable operating leases can be a form of off-balance-sheet financing, which distorts the traditional measures of leverage and profitability. Substantially all of International Paper's leases are capital leases, which appear on the balance sheet as part of long-term debt. The items leased are included in plants, properties, and equipment.

A horizontal analysis of the common-size statements reveals which items show marked changes in importance. The marked changes in International Paper's balance sheet include decreases in the relative importance of retained earnings and, as a result, total shareholders' equity. Long-term debt gained in importance in 1990, but has fallen back to its 1989 share since then. Short-term debt has gained in importance since 1990, boosting the relative shares of current liabilities and total liabilities.

The primary tools of horizontal analysis are annual percent changes, the rightmost set of columns in the sample analysis, and trend percentages. Also called index numbers, trend percentages express each line item as a percentage of its amount in a base year, 1989 in this example. The middle set of columns on the right-hand page of the sample analysis presents trend percentages. There is no column of trend percentages for 1989 because every entry would be 100. These calculations confirm that long-term debt did increase sharply in 1990, but that its declining importance since then in the common-size balance sheet has reflected steady growth in total assets as much as it has the 1992 decrease in long-term debt. Similarly, the waning importance of retained earnings is attributable almost entirely to growth in total assets. The increasing importance of short-term debt, however, does reflect the rapid growth of that line item, rather than the trend of total assets.

This cursory horizontal analysis reveals a shortcoming of common-size

24

statements: they can obscure significant trends in line items, especially those items that are small fractions of the benchmark quantity. To observe that cash increased from 1 percent of assets in 1989 to 2 percent in 1990 does not have the same impact as observing a 151 percent increase or observing an increase in the trend percentage from 100 to 251. In fact, the percent changes and trend percentages suggest some important questions for the analyst to apply to the audited notes to the financial statements and to management's discussion and analysis. Why did cash and other current assets more than double in 1990? Why did goodwill, deferred charges, and other assets also jump in that year? Why did investments plunge in 1990 and rebound as sharply in 1991 and 1992?

On the liabilities side, what accounts for the substantial increase in short-term debt over the past 2 years, and does that increase pose any threat to the company's solvency? Why did minority interest and other liabilities increase sharply in 1990 and 1991? Were those increases related to the volatility in investments? How many layoffs does the 20 percent drop in 1992 payroll represent? How has the company employed the proceeds of its 1992 stock offering and its sales of treasury stock?

Unlike common-size statements, which can understate changes in some items, percent changes suffer from the drawback of exaggerating temporary declines in line items. An excellent example of this problem is the 1990 and 1991 changes in International Paper's investments. The $364 million 1990 decrease in this line item amounted to a 78 percent decrease, but the $280 million 1991 rebound was an increase of *272 percent*. Analysts should be particularly attentive to this drawback when working with quarterly data, which tend to be subject to sharp seasonal variations. The use of 4-quarter percent changes is a common way of handling this problem because 4-quarter changes compare periods subject to the same seasonal factors. A related drawback of using percent changes is the problem of interpreting a percent change from a positive value to a negative value and *vice versa*. The sample analysis shows no percent changes for working capital because this item fell from $404 million at year-end 1991 to *negative* $165 million at the end of 1992.

The advantage of using trend percentages is that they can put sharp fluctuations in perspective, given a reasonable choice of base year. Compare these two methods of measuring the changes in International Paper's investments:

	1989	1990	1991	1992
Trend percentages	100	22	82	128
Annual percent changes	--	-77.9	271.8	56.4

For most line items on this company's balance sheet, 1989 is a suitable choice of base year because it was the last full year of the 1982-90 business-cycle expansion. Recession years, 1990 and 1991 in this example, often are poor base years because some items fall abnormally low, exaggerating subsequent percent changes. In the sample analysis, 1990 would be a poor base year for computing trend percentages in investments. Using one base year for every line item also poses some problems. The best base year for computing trend percentages in International Paper's cash and temporary investments is 1991:

	1989	1990	1991	1992
Cash and temporary investments, at cost	43	108	100	95

Ratio Analysis

There are many useful comparisons to be made within a set of balance sheets beyond observing the changes in each line item and computing each line item as a fraction of total assets. Ratio analysis is the name applied to comparisons that have achieved some popularity as guides to an enterprise's financial condition. Ratios computed solely from balance sheet data are among the oldest such comparisons, because the balance sheet has long been the most readily available financial disclosure. Because these ratios reflect the information requirements and disclosure practices of an earlier era, the ongoing evolution of business and accounting practices is reducing the relevance of many traditional measures. People still discuss balance sheet ratios, however, so we present some commonly encountered ratios below.

Just like the dollar values in a financial statement, ratios beg the question, "Compared to what?" An enterprise's financial ratios afford two types of comparison: the comparison of each ratio to its previous values to determine a trend, and comparison of ratios to those of comparable enterprises and to industry averages. The sample analysis of International Paper's balance sheets includes 4 years of data for each ratio to reveal any recent trends. The sample analysis does not include data for peer and industry comparisons. The main sources for these comparative data are:

Key Business Ratios (New York: Dun & Bradstreet, Inc., annual).

Annual Statement Studies (Philadelphia: Robert Morris Associates, annual).

Industry Surveys (New York: Standard & Poor's Corporation, annual).

Troy, Leo, *Almanac of Business and Industrial Financial Ratios* (Englewood Cliffs, NJ: Prentice-Hall, annual).

There are many other sources of comparative ratio data, including trade and industry association reports, other publications of commercial financial reporting services, and government publications. Many of these organizations also offer ratio data and the underlying financial statement data to computer users *via* on-line and CD-ROM services.

The current ratio is perhaps the most widely reported balance-sheet ratio.

(1) current ratio = current assets ÷ current liabilities

This is a measure of an enterprise's short-term solvency. A higher current ratio indicates a greater likelihood that an enterprise can meet its obligations promptly. Given a reasonable assurance of solvency, a high or increasing current ratio is not an improvement in an enterprise's financial position, because it suggests an inefficient use of current assets. A 2:1 ratio once had an almost religious significance as the benchmark for a sound current position, but as is the case with any ratio, a useful interpretation requires comparisons with past results and with the ratios of comparable enterprises.

A similar approach to gauging solvency with balance sheet data is to compute working capital:

(2) working capital = current assets – current liabilities

Unlike the current ratio, this measure is dollar denominated, therefore it is not useful for comparisons among enterprises. The trend of working capital and its size as a fraction of total assets complement the information that the current ratio provides.

As discussed on page 13, the assets that a balance sheet advertises as current are not usually all of an enterprise's current assets, nor are they entirely current. Similarly, current liabilities and liabilities alleged to be current are not always identical. These misleading classifications impair the usefulness of the current ratio and of working capital as indicators of solvency. One method of coping with this problem is to take a conservative approach to measuring the assets available to meet short-term obligations.

(3) quick assets = cash and temporary investments + receivables

(4) quick assets ratio = quick assets ÷ current liabilities

The use of quick assets and the quick assets ratio, also called the acid-test ratio, recognizes that inventories and other current assets take considerable time and effort to convert to cash, so that they usually are not available to pay debts due immediately. This distinction is based on the quality of assets, which is a combination of liquidity and the likelihood that recorded values will be realized in a liquidation.

The recognition of differences in the quality of assets addresses only a portion of the problem with current classifications, however. It ignores

27

long-term receivables and uncollectible accounts, the current portion of fixed assets, readily saleable inventory, and the maturity distribution of current liabilities. The basic difficulty in using the balance sheet to assess solvency is that it does not provide all of the relevant information. Solvency is mainly a question of cash flows. When doubts about the adequacy of cash *balances* arise, it probably is too late for corrective action. For further discussion of solvency analysis, see Chapter V on receivables and inventory turnover and Chapter VII on cash flows.

The best that can be said for the balance sheet solvency measures is that if they are unfavorable, they alert the analyst to the need for careful scrutiny of more relevant measures.

$	366 $	784 $	404 $	(165) Working Capital (current assets less current liabilities)
	1.13	1.25	1.11	0.96 Current Ratio
	0.59	0.65	0.56	0.46 Quick Assets Ratio

International Paper's low and deteriorating current ratio, its deteriorating quick assets ratio, and its negative working capital position are red flags, signaling to the analyst the importance of examining the company's turnover ratios and its cash flow from operations.

In contrast with the problems of using the balance sheet in solvency analysis, the balance sheet is not fundamentally ill-suited for analyzing a business's capital structure; it is designed to reveal that structure. A basic analysis of a business's capital structure involves a comparison of the relative proportions of the elements of equity and of long-term debt within the balance sheet, with reference to recent trends and industry averages. Many analysts use this approach as a starting point, computing the following ratios:

(5)   debt ratio = total liabilities ÷ total assets

(6)   debt-equity ratio = total liabilities ÷ equity

(7)   capitalization ratio = $\dfrac{\text{long-term liabilities}}{\text{long-term liabilities} + \text{equity}}$

One additional ratio, that of long-term liabilities to equity, is self-explanatory. Some analysts prefer to compute these ratios from the stockholder's point of view, by substituting equity for total liabilities in Equation (5) and for long-term liabilities in the numerator of Equation (7), and by inverting Equation (6) and the ratio of long-term liabilities to equity.

Whatever the calculations, analysts use these ratios to answer this question: "How are the outstanding claims on the assets of the business apportioned among creditors, especially long-term creditors, and own-

28

ers?" In International Paper's case, leverage increased sharply from 1989 through 1991 and moderately in 1992.

| 0.56 | 0.59 | 0.62 | 0.62 | Debt Ratio |
| 1.25 | 1.43 | 1.60 | 1.66 | Debt-Equity Ratio |

Long-term leverage fell slightly in 1992 as the company issued additional stock and substituted substantial amounts of short-term borrowing for long-term debt.

| 0.42 | 0.46 | 0.49 | 0.48 | Capitalization Ratio |
| 0.72 | 0.87 | 0.95 | 0.93 | Ratio of Long-Term Liabilities to Equity |

Equations (5), (6), and (7) convey a false air of precision. For clarity, we have used "debt" as a synonym for total liabilities. In practice, "debt" is used to describe a variety of quantities, ranging from long-term debt plus notes payable to total liabilities less minority interest, plus redeemable preferred stock and a large fraction or all of noncapitalized financial leases. Long-term liabilities may or may not include the current portion of long-term debt, depending on the analyst. We have excluded the current portion. In addition, the equity figure used in ratio analysis may differ markedly from reported total shareholders' equity. Possible additions to the reported total include obligations not likely to be paid, such as minority interest and a portion of deferred income taxes, and unrealized gains on assets, such as the excess of FIFO inventory valuations over LIFO valuations and the excess of the market value of investments over cost.

A common way for companies to reduce their reported leverage is the "50 percent solution," which refers to a method of off-balance-sheet financing. Fifty percent is the threshold ownership interest at which consolidation requirements take effect. By holding just under 50 percent of a heavily indebted affiliate, a company can report its holding as an investment while still exercising effective control, thereby avoiding the disclosure of a substantial amount of leverage. Some companies even spin off business lines to take advantage of this possibility. Analysts usually do not have enough pertinent information available to adjust debt measures to reflect this practice, but they should be alert to its presence.

An alternative approach to the analysis of a publicly traded corporation's capital structure is to compare the market value of equity to the value that the balance sheet reports. The advantage of this approach, especially for the inexperienced analyst, is that it relies on the collective judgment of thousands of self-interested marketplace participants. The comparison can be on an aggregate basis or on a per-share basis. The relevant equations are:

(8) book value per common share = equity ÷ common shares issued

(9) market value of equity = stock price × common shares outstanding

In Equation (8), equity is common shareholders' equity, which is the par value of common stock plus paid-in capital plus retained earnings net of the liquidation value of preferred stock plus the foreign currency translation adjustment, if present. If there are substantial amounts of warrants, options, stock purchase rights, or convertible senior securities outstanding, the analyst should adjust for the potential dilution from these sources. There usually is no adjustment for treasury stock or ESOP stock in this calculation, so the per-share measure is book value per common share issued. If the corporation holds substantial amounts of treasury stock, it may be appropriate to compute book value per common share outstanding in order to compare per-share market price and book value.

The comparison of book value to market value indicates the degree to which asset values according to the various accounting rules differ from their values in service, as appraised in the marketplace. The use of market valuations has two important disadvantages. First, a corporation's equity has no fixed value; its price can change by the minute when the stock market is open. Second, market values reflect the availability and scarcity of funds as much as they do the service values of corporate net assets. During periods of speculation, investors' sole valuation principle tends to be the expectation of what future purchasers, hopefully flush with cash, will be willing to pay for a corporation's stock.

INTERNATIONAL PAPER COMPANY
Consolidated Statement of Earnings (Multiple Step)
For the Year Ended December 31, 1992

(in millions, except per share amounts)

Net Sales		$13,598
Cost of Products Sold		10,137
Gross Profit on Sales		$ 3,461
Operating Expenses:		
Depreciation and amortization	$850	
Distribution expenses	629	
Selling and administrative expenses	981	
Taxes other than payroll and income taxes	150	
Productivity improvement charge	398	
Total Operating Expenses, excluding income taxes		3,008
Earnings from Operations, before income taxes		$ 453
Interest Expense, net		247
Earnings before Income Taxes, Extraordinary Item, *and Cumulative Effect of Accounting Changes*		$ 206
Provision for Income Taxes		64
Earnings before Extraordinary Item *and Cumulative Effect of Accounting Changes*		$ 142
Extraordinary Item — loss on extinguishment of debt (less tax benefit of $3)		(6)
Cumulative Effect of Change in Accounting for Income Taxes		(50)
Net Earnings		$ 86
Weighted Average Common Shares Outstanding		121.4
Earnings per Common Share:		
Earnings before extraordinary item and cumulative effect of accounting changes		$1.17
Extraordinary item — loss on extinguishment of debt		(0.05)
Cumulative effect of change in accounting for income taxes		(0.41)
Earnings per Common Share		**$0.71**

This multiple-step statement and the single-step statement on page 34 have been adapted from *International Paper Annual Report for 1992* (Purchase, NY: International Paper Company, 1993), p. 42. The notes on pp. 46-52 of the *Annual Report* are an integral part of the original statement.

IV.

THE INCOME STATEMENT

Income twenty shillings — expenditures nineteen shillings and sixpence — result, Happiness.

Income twenty shillings — expenditures twenty shillings and sixpence — result, Misery.

– Wilkins Micawber (Dickens)

AN income statement reconciles an enterprise's revenues, expenses, gains, and losses for an accounting period, and states the total of those items. The total goes by many names, including earnings, net income, comprehensive income, change in fund balances, and change in net assets. An income statement accounts for the changes in an enterprise's net assets that do not result from transactions with owners or donors between successive balance sheet dates. Synonyms for income statement include statement of operations, results of operations, statement of profit and loss, and statement of earnings, but this list is not exhaustive. The mark of the Wall Streeter is his use of the abbreviation "P&L" for "statement of profit and loss."

Income statements come in two formats: single step and multiple step. A single-step statement calculates earnings from operations by subtracting total costs and expenses from total revenues. An example appears on page 34. A multiple-step statement first determines gross profit on sales (step 1) and then subtracts operating expenses (step 2) to arrive at operating earnings. Only merchandising enterprises (manufacturers, wholesalers, and retailers) use the multiple-step format, which appears at left, because gross profit is not a useful measure for service enterprises — all of their sales are gross profit. Corporate income statements include an additional feature, the computation of earnings per share before and after adjustments for extraordinary items. A sample calculation of earnings per share appears at left.

Accountants classify earnings by source, just as they distinguish between earnings as a whole and funds provided by owners or donors. The cash receipts that an enterprise's principal activities generate are revenues. The cash payments arising from those activities are expenses. The difference between revenue and expenses is earnings from operations. Gains and losses are the cash flows resulting from transactions and events that are incidental to, or simply not among, an enterprise's principal activities. Gains net of losses constitute nonoperating earnings. The sum of nonoperating and operating earnings is net earnings, often called net income.

That said, the items labeled revenue, expenses, gains, and losses in financial statements do not always conform to this classification, which is drawn from the FASB's "conceptual framework."* Income statements often label negative operating earnings as "operating loss," for example, even though the negative earnings stem from an enterprise's principal activities. In addition, income statements label net interest receipts or payments and certain other nonoperating items as revenues and expenses. The productivity improvement charge on International Paper's 1992 income statement provides another example of labeling inconsistent with the conceptual framework. The notes to the financial statements reveal that this charge is predominantly a write-down of assets associated with plant shutdowns — a loss, in other words, although it appears in the list of expenses.

Accrual Accounting

Revenues, expenses, gains, and losses all consist of cash flows (or equivalent transactions, in which no cash changes hands, that affect asset

---

* Specifically, the FASB's "Statement of Financial Accounting Concepts No. 6: Elements of Financial Statements," *Financial Accounting Series* (December 1985), No. 17, pp. 29-32.

INTERNATIONAL PAPER COMPANY
Consolidated Statement of Earnings (Single Step)
For the Year Ended December 31, 1992

(in millions, except per share amounts)

Net Sales		$13,598
Costs and Expenses:		
Cost of products sold	$10,137	
Depreciation and amortization	850	
Distribution expenses	629	
Selling and administrative expenses	981	
Taxes other than payroll and income taxes	150	
Productivity improvement charge	398	
Total Costs and Expenses		13,145
Earnings before Interest, Income Taxes, Extraordinary Item,		
and Cumulative Effect of Accounting Changes		$ 453
Interest Expense, net		247
Earnings before Income Taxes, Extraordinary Item,		
and Cumulative Effect of Accounting Changes		$ 206
Provision for Income Taxes		64
Earnings before Extraordinary Item and Cumulative		
Effect of Accounting Changes		$ 142
Extraordinary Item — loss on extinguishment of debt (less tax benefit of $3)		(6)
Cumulative Effect of Change in Accounting for Income Taxes		(50)
Net Earnings		$ 86

and liability accounts), but the cash flows do not always coincide with the recognition of these four elements of earnings. Enterprises may record expenses for the current period that reflect cash payments made many years ago. They may record losses to account for estimated impairments of asset values during the current period. Such losses reflect prospective reductions in future cash flows. Similarly, cash receipts may precede or follow revenue-generating sales and services.

The reason for these differences in timing is that cash flows can be a poor short-term indicator of an enterprise's performance. A steep decline in cash flows from operations from the fourth quarter to first quarter may not be cause for concern if the business reporting the decline is a department store or a toy store. Contractors on a long-term construction project might receive a large down payment, no cash receipts for more than a year, and then a large final payment. Not all enterprises have irregular operating cash flows — such flows might be a crucial indicator of, say, a supermarket's month-to-month performance — but even these enterprises incur gains and losses that affect performance but are incidental to regular operations.

Short-term results provide an enterprise's managers with information that is crucial for successful operations. The imperfections of cash flow as a measure of short-term results led long ago to the development of accrual accounting, which consists of the generally accepted accounting principles used to assign portions of cash flows to the revenues, expenses, gains, and losses of more than one accounting period. Earnings, the end product of accrual accounting, have proven to be a useful short-term performance measure for managers and other interested parties.

The two key principles of accrual accounting are the realization principle and the matching principle. Under the realization principle, enterprises record revenues when they deliver goods or provide services. Under the matching principle, enterprises attempt to allocate expenses among all periods in which those expenses contribute to revenues. Matching is hardly a science — it involves a considerable reliance on estimates, predictions, and arbitrary judgments. Taken together, the two principles require enterprises to compute operating earnings for a period as the revenue from goods and services provided during the period, net of the expenses directly attributable to producing that revenue, and net of a systematic allocation of expenses not directly associated with the volume of revenue for any one period.

There are two techniques for applying these principles: accrual and deferral. Accrual is the process of recognizing future cash flows as revenues or expenses in the current period. Accrued expenses become liabilities until paid, and accrued revenues become assets until received. Accounts receivable and payable are examples of accrued assets and liabilities.

Deferral is the opposite of accrual; it is the process of assigning current cash flows to the revenues and expenses of future periods. Deferred expenses become assets until charged against earnings, and deferred revenues become liabilities until earned. In the case of cash outlays for acquiring equipment and other long-lived assets, an enterprise charges portions of each outlay to expenses over the estimated useful lives of the assets, thereby deferring the recognition of the initial outlays as expenses. In the case of cash receipts for goods and services to be provided for several periods, such as subscriptions, an enterprise records the receipts as liabilities and credits a portion of each receipt to revenue as it provides those goods and services.

The income statement reveals the principles and techniques of accrual accounting at work:

Net Sales	$13,598
Cost of Products Sold	10,137
Gross Profit on Sales	$ 3,461

The gross profit calculation involves the use of the realization principle to determine net sales, and the matching principle to determine the cost of products sold. Like any other merchandising business, International Paper defers the recognition of cash outlays for production and purchasing costs by recording those outlays as assets, namely inventories. As the company makes sales, it earns the revenues that result from its inventory outlays, so it must charge matching expenses against those revenues. The company does so by transferring the portion of inventories attributable to sales to an expense account, cost of products sold.

The difference between net sales and cost of products sold is gross profit, rather than net profit (earnings), because the company must match many other expenses against sales revenues:

Gross Profit on Sales		$ 3,461
Operating Expenses:		
Depreciation and amortization	$850	
Distribution expenses	629	
Selling and administrative expenses	981	
Taxes other than payroll and income taxes	150	
Productivity improvement charge	398	
Total Operating Expenses, excluding income taxes		3,008
Earnings from Operations, before income taxes		$ 453

Most of the amounts of distribution expenses and selling and administrative expenses are accruals. Until paid, these amounts appear on the balance sheet as liabilities, including accounts payable and accrued payroll and benefits. In contrast, depreciation and amortization are important examples of deferral. Using these techniques, the company charges a portion of cash outlays for fixed assets against revenue for the period.

Because of the difficulties of determining how much any particular long-lived asset contributes to the revenue of each period, an enterprise usually determines depreciation and amortization according to arbitrary formulas based on the volume of production or the passage of time in relation to the asset's expected useful life. The notes to International Paper's financial statements disclose the particular types of formulas that the company uses. Depreciation and amortization do not include depletion of forestlands, because that expense can be matched against revenue as part of the cost of products sold.

The income statements of most enterprises list interest revenue and expense, or net interest, separately from the operating items. The reason for this classification is that interest expense accrues from financing activities and interest revenue accrues from investing activities. With few exceptions, only financial companies count financing and investing as operating activities. For most other enterprises, those activities are incidental to operations. Even major conglomerates such as ITT Corporation and General Electric, which some analysts have compared to mutual funds, list net interest separately. From the creditor's point of view, the advantage of this separate listing is that the margin by which an enterprise's current operations fund interest payments is readily apparent.

A corporation's provision for income taxes is a combination of accruals and deferrals. The accruals reflect the usual practice of paying taxes in the current period on taxable income earned in the previous period. The deferrals reflect the myriad differences between GAAP earnings and taxable income. Profitable corporations normally report a positive deferral component of the provision for income taxes and a growing net deferred tax liability. Because of the peculiarities of tax allocation, deferred tax liabilities and deferred tax assets both appear on corporate balance sheets (the assets often are lumped together with other current assets). Corporate income statements show just the net provision for income taxes, however, although the notes to the financial statements usually disclose various components of the provision.

Technically, the portion of a corporation's provision for income taxes that is attributable to operating items is an operating expense and it should appear in the list of operating expenses, so that the income statement presents earnings from operations net of tax. In practice, corporate income statements present income taxes among the nonoperating items and they do not disclose the amount of taxes attributable to operating items. The provision for income taxes includes the tax consequences of items that appear below the provision on the income statement. The income statement lists these line items net of tax, but it includes disclosures of their tax consequences.

Three categories of line items can follow the provision for income taxes on the income statement: earnings from discontinued operations, extraordinary items, and the cumulative effect of changes in accounting principles. Discontinued operations include entire business lines or subsidiaries that an enterprise has sold or liquidated. Plant closings and other reorganizations are unusual items, *not* discontinued operations. Unusual items are components of operating earnings, which often are called earnings from continuing operations. International Paper's productivity improvement charge is an unusual item; the company did not have any discontinued operations in 1992.

When an enterprise decides to discontinue operations, it separates the earnings of those operations on all income statements prepared after the decision. Comparative income statements also separate earnings of the discontinued operations in previous periods. The income statement for the period in which operations end, which may lag considerably the decision to discontinue, shows gains or losses on the disposal of the operations plus any earnings for the final period.

Extraordinary items must meet three criteria to qualify for separate presentation: they must be material, unusual, and not expected to recur in the foreseeable future. Examples of items that qualify as extraordinary include losses from natural disasters, wars, and riots, and the effects of government expropriations and condemnations, major changes in law, and major changes in financial conditions. The last example includes the precipitous drop in interest rates since 1989, which prompted International Paper to retire high-coupon bonds at a loss in order to refinance at lower rates:

Extraordinary Item — loss on extinguishment of debt (less tax benefit of $3)   (6)

When an enterprise changes the accounting principles that it uses, it calculates the difference the change would have made in the earnings of past accounting periods and charges the cumulative sum of those changes against current-period earnings. The most common reason for changing accounting principles is to comply with a new *Statement of Financial Accounting Standards* (SFAS). Other reasons include voluntary changes, such as choosing a new inventory valuation method or depreciation method, and changes in GAAP set forth by organizations other than the FASB, such as the SEC or the AICPA.

The cumulative effects of changes in accounting principles have been major items on corporate income statements in recent years. The 1992 adjustment to International Paper's earnings is a case in point — it amounts to more than a third of the company's after-tax earnings. This adjustment reflects the adoption of SFAS number 109, which requires corporations to change certain tax allocation practices. Another important adjustment was for SFAS 106, which was extraordinary even for an extraordinary item. This *Statement* required businesses to change from a cash basis to an accrual basis of accounting for retirees' health care plans and other postretirement benefits. The adjustment amounted to a $215 million charge against International Paper's 1991 after-tax earnings of $399 million. For IBM, the charge was $2.3 billion on top of a 1991 after-tax loss of $598 million. General Electric reported a $1.8 billion dollar charge against 1991 after-tax earnings of $4.4 billion, including discontinued operations.

Net earnings are what remains after a business has deducted extraordinary items, earnings from discontinued operations, and the effects of accounting changes from after-tax earnings. This is the so-called "bottom line." Its significance is that it is the amount available to those with an equity interest in the business. A business attracts equity investment with the prospect of positive and growing earnings. Businesses that incur persistent net losses eventually go bankrupt. Thus the amount and trend of net earnings are critical evidence of management's ability to maintain a business, to fund growth internally, and to provide adequate returns to investors.

Earnings per Share

It is a commonplace to call net earnings the bottom line, but corporate income statements include some important lines below net earnings. These lines present earnings per common share, often called earnings per share.

Net Earnings	**$ 86**
Weighted Average Common Shares Outstanding	121.4
Earnings per Common Share:	
Earnings before extraordinary item and cumulative effect of accounting changes	$1.17
Extraordinary item — loss on extinguishment of debt	(0.05)
Cumulative effect of change in accounting for income taxes	(0.41)
Earnings per Common Share	**$0.71**

When there are preferred shares outstanding, the earnings per share presentation includes an additional step, the computation of earnings applicable to common shares, which is the difference between net earnings and preferred dividend requirements.

39

From the investor's point of view, earnings per share is a more useful figure than net earnings because it measures the investor's *pro rata* share of earnings, which varies with the number of shares outstanding. Professional analysts compute the present value of estimated future per-share earnings to determine whether a corporation's shares warrant a buy, hold, or sell rating at current market prices. The rationale for this calculation is that if the present value of a corporation's earnings per share exceeds the current market price, the market price is a bargain and the shares warrant a buy rating. This process is, of course, only as good as the earnings estimates that go into it.

Earnings per share is a more complicated measure than book value per share because the number of shares outstanding varies during most accounting periods, whereas the number of issued shares at the end of any accounting period is fixed. Corporations that have relatively simple capital structures divide earnings for an accounting period by the weighted average number of shares outstanding during the period to compute earnings per share. The use of the weighted average adjusts for variations in the number of outstanding shares. An example of a simple capital structure is a corporation that has issued nonconvertible bonds, nonconvertible preferred shares, and one class of common shares.

Relatively complex capital structures can include convertible preferred issues, convertible bonds, warrants, options, and a variety of more exotic securities. When the holders of these types of securities convert them to common shares for a consideration that is below the market price, the conversions dilute the interests of current holders of common shares. Participation certificates and multiple classes of common stock also complicate capital structures because of the sharing of earnings and dividend participation that these arrangements require.

Widespread failure to recognize these forms of dilution of earnings participation fueled the merger craze of the late 1960s, as growing conglomerates issued convertible securities to make acquisitions. These transactions amounted to deferred issuances of common shares to buy the current earnings of acquisitions. Failure to account for dilution from future conversions allowed the acquiring corporations to report growing earnings per share.

This type of distortion led to the requirement that corporations for which earnings per common share, as described above, is subject to a reduction of more than 3 percent due to dilution must present primary and fully diluted earnings per share instead. These two measures account for the effects of dilution using slightly different assumptions about dilutive transactions. Knowledge of the complex calculations involved is best left to the accountants; it suffices to understand that fully diluted earnings per share is the more conservative measure, and that shareholders of corporations that do not disclose the effects of dilution in audited financial statements risk no more than a 3 percent dilution of their interests.

Statements of Equity and Net Assets

The income statement does not provide a complete accounting of the changes in an enterprise's financial position. It does not account for the disposition of net earnings or for the enterprise's transactions with owners or donors. The statement that accounts for these items depends on the enterprise's form of organization: for corporations, it is the statement of shareholders' equity; for partnerships, the statement of partners' equity; for sole proprietorships, the statement of owner's equity; for nonprofit enterprises, the statement of changes in net assets, commonly called the statement of changes in fund balances.

Some corporations present just a statement of retained earnings, which is less comprehensive than the statement of shareholders' equity. Whatever its name, the statement is with few exceptions just a bookkeeping document, of little significance to the analyst. General Electric relegated its 1992 statement of shareholders' equity to the notes to its financial statements.

A statement of owner's, partners,' or shareholders' equity accounts for the changes in a business's equity position during an accounting period. Sources of increases in equity include net earnings if positive, additional investments by shareholders or principals, and, rarely, donations. Additional investments by a corporation's shareholders can include indirect forms of investment, such as sales of treasury stock, conversions of senior securities, and distributions of ESOP stock. Similarly, the sources of increase in the net assets of a nonprofit enterprise include donations and positive net earnings. Net losses and payments to investors reduce a business's equity, and net losses reduce a nonprofit enterprise's net assets. Indirect payments to a corporation's investors, such as purchases of treasury stock and ESOP stock, can reduce equity. Foreign currency translation adjustments can produce both reductions and increases in a corporation's equity.

One important difference between a statement of owner's or partners' equity and a statement of shareholders' equity is that payments to principals are called drawings rather than dividends. Another important difference is that net earnings accumulate in the principals' capital accounts rather than in retained earnings. Statements of partners' equity can be highly complex, depending on the provisions of the partnership agreement.

41

INTERNATIONAL PAPER
Consolidated Statement of Common Shareholders' Equity

(in millions, except share amounts in thousands and ratios)	Common Stock Issued		Paid-In Capital*	Retained Earnings	Treasury Stock		Total Common Shareholders' Equity	Dividend Payout Ratio
	Shares	Amount			Shares	Amount		
Balance, January 1, 1990	116,988	$117	$1,161	$4,195	8,276	$326	$5,147	0.32
Issuance of stock for various plans	315		37		(682)	(17)	54	
Cash dividends — common stock ($1.68 per share)				(183)			(183)	
Foreign currency translation (less tax benefit of $23)			45				45	
Net earnings				569			569	
Balance, December 31, 1990	117,303	$117	$1,243	$4,581	7,594	$309	$5,632	1.01
Conversion of subordinated debentures			33		(1,244)	(43)	76	
Issuance of stock for merger			(7)	13	(512)	(13)	19	
Issuance of stock for various plans	275	1	39		(714)	(18)	58	
Cash dividends — common stock ($1.68 per share)				(186)			(186)	
Foreign currency translation (less tax benefit of $10)			(44)				(44)	
Net earnings				184			184	
Balance, December 31, 1991	117,578	$118	$1,264	$4,592	5,124	$235	$5,739	2.40
Issuance of stock in a public offering	9,200	9	641				650	
Issuance of stock for various plans	215		27		(793)	(33)	60	
Cash dividends — common stock ($1.68 per share)				(206)			(206)	
Foreign currency translation (less tax benefit of $58)			(140)				(140)	
Net earnings				86			86	
Balance, December 31, 1992	**126,993**	**$127**	**$1,792**	**$4,472**	**4,331**	**$202**	**$6,189**	

*The cumulative foreign currency translation adjustment was $(152) million, $(12) million and $32 million at December 31, 1992, 1991 and 1990, respectively.

Adapted from *International Paper Annual Report for 1992* (Purchase, NY: International Paper Company, 1993), p. 45. The notes on pp. 46-52 of the *Annual Report* are an integral part of the original statement.

Although daunting in appearance, as the example at left shows, a corporation's statement of shareholders' equity usually is straightforward. The pertinent items for the analyst and for the investor are the per-share dividend (often reported on the income statement) and the dividend payout ratio, which is the ratio of total common-stock dividend payments to net earnings applicable to common shares. A ratio between 0 and 1 indicates an increase in retained earnings and suggests the degree to which the corporation can finance expanded operations without issuing stock or borrowing. A ratio less than 0 indicates that the corporation is using retained earnings to cover losses and pay dividends. A ratio greater than 1 indicates the use of retained earnings to supplement net earnings as a source of dividends.

A nonprofit enterprise's statement of changes in net assets usually follows the matrix format of the statement of shareholders' equity. Just as the shareholders' equity statement discloses the changes of each element of equity stemming from each type of transaction, so the change in net assets statement shows the effect of each transaction on the net assets of each fund. The net assets of each fund commonly are called fund balances. An important difference between nonprofit accounting and business accounting is that some nonprofit enterprises present a statement of current-fund operations rather than a consolidated income statement. These enterprises incorporate the consolidated income statement into the statement of changes in net assets.

43

V.

ANALYSIS OF THE INCOME STATEMENT

A S with the balance sheet, vertical, horizontal, and ratio analyses are the essential procedures for analyzing the income statement. Chapter III discusses the basics of those procedures. They are essential for analyzing *any* financial disclosure because they help the analyst answer the question, "Compared to what?"

Vertical analysis of the income statement has many limitations as a guide to a business's performance. The common-size income statement reveals some important measures of profitability, but not all of them, and it can only hint at a business's solvency. Vertical analysis is useful as a first step, however, because it reveals which aspects of a business's performance deserve careful attention as the analysis proceeds.

Net sales are the benchmark quantity for a vertical analysis of the income statement, so the common-size income statement lists each item as a decimal fraction of net sales. The sample analysis of International Paper's income statement, which appears after page 47,* reveals three key fractions: the cost of products sold consumes as much as three-fourths of sales revenue; other operating expenses consume two-thirds or more of the remainder; net earnings have amounted to 10 percent of net sales in recent years, at most. These proportions vary widely from firm to firm, but International Paper's are typical for a manufacturing business because its cost of products sold consumes the overwhelming majority of revenues, while only a tiny fraction remains for shareholders.

Profit Margins

The fraction of net sales remaining after deducting the cost of products sold is a business's gross profit margin, a key measure of profitability. There are no net earnings without gross profits, barring extraordinary nonoperating gains. A business's gross profit margin indicates its average rate of profit per dollar of sales, which provides a basis for forecasting how much a change in sales volume would affect earnings. Using International Paper's 1992 gross profit margin, one can forecast that each additional dollar of sales revenue will yield 25 cents to cover operating expenses and provide a return to investors.

The size of the gross profit margin also is important as an indicator of the amount of volume a business must generate in order to earn a net profit. If operating expenses are relatively stable over a range of sales volumes, it

---

* Having photocopies of these four pages at hand will make the discussion of the sample analysis easier to follow.

takes more volume to generate a given amount of net profit with a low-margin product than with a comparably priced high-margin product. Cost pressures are thus more intense for managers of low-margin businesses.

The multiple-step income statement at the beginning of Chapter IV and the sample analysis of International Paper's income statement in this chapter both present gross profit as the difference between net sales and the cost of products sold. This formula technically is correct, but the company does not include depreciation of plant and equipment in its measure of the cost of products sold, so our adaptation of its published single-step income statement to the multiple-step format overstates the company's gross profit and gross profit margin.

One way to correct for this overstatement is to add depreciation and amortization to the cost of products sold:

(fractions of net sales)	1989	1990	1991	1992
Gross profit on sales	0.30	0.29	0.27	0.25
Less: Depreciation and amortization	0.05	0.05	0.06	0.06
Adjusted gross profit margin	0.25	0.24	0.21	0.19

This adjustment has some drawbacks: a portion of depreciation and amortization relates to corporate headquarters and other nonproduction facilities, so it does not belong in production costs; also, some of the depreciation that is attributable to production costs should be allocated to inventory, because not all products produced during an accounting period are sold. These qualifications are small compared to the totals involved, however, so the adjusted gross profit margin is somewhat more accurate than the gross margin reported in the common-size statement.

The gross profit margin is just one of several measures of profitability on the common-size income statement. The operating margin, which is earnings from operations as a percentage of sales, is another such measure. Earnings from operations add fixed costs to the variable costs considered in the gross profit calculation, thus measuring the overall profitability of operations for a given period. Because earnings from operations include fixed costs, the operating margin is not as useful a measure of unit profitability as the gross margin; the operating margin is more likely to change as the volume of sales changes. As a measure of the overall efficiency of operations, however, the operating margin is more useful than the gross profit margin.

From the shareholder's or principal's point of view, pretax earnings (earnings before income taxes, extraordinary item, and the cumulative effect of accounting changes) and the pretax profit margin are the most relevant measures of profitability. First, pretax earnings reflect the deduction of net interest expense from operating earnings. Net interest can consume a sizeable fraction of the operating margin if a business employs leverage. If so, the operating margin does not include all of the information relevant to an assessment of management's performance. A common reason for using leverage is to purchase productive assets in order to increase earnings. A complete assessment of management's effectiveness at using leverage must include the cost of leverage, which is net interest expense.

Second, pretax earnings is more relevant than net earnings, which often include extraordinary items beyond management's control. A case in point is the $215 million charge against International Paper's 1991 earnings for the cumulative effect of a change in accounting principle. This FASB-mandated charge amounted to $1.95 per share, a deduction of 2 percent of net sales from an after-tax margin of 3 percent. Despite its size, the charge was essentially a bookkeeping adjustment to the retained earnings account; it was irrelevant to an assessment of management's 1991 performance.

Third, corporate managements enjoy a degree of flexibility in determining the provision for income taxes. Because of this flexibility, management's ability to conduct transactions in ways that minimize the corporate tax burden strongly influences reported after-tax earnings. This ability is important, but shareholders and analysts should consider it separately from management's ability to produce a return on the resources entrusted to it.

Fourth, the provision for income taxes typically includes a substantial deferred component that reflects the change in a corporation's deferred tax liabilities, not its current tax obligations. Due to the conservative bias of tax allocation practices, deferred tax liabilities can include substantial amounts that are unlikely ever to be paid to tax authorities. This conservatism has produced ever-increasing deferred tax liabilities on many corporate balance sheets, so that deferred taxes have become a form of "stealth equity." To the extent that the provision for income taxes includes such permanent deferrals, pretax earnings is more relevant than after-tax earnings as a measure of management's ability to preserve and increase a corporation's equity.

Horizontal Analysis

By all measures, International Paper's earnings plunged between 1989 and 1992. Net earnings in 1992 amounted to 10 percent of its 1989 level, having fallen by two-thirds from 1990 to 1991 and by more than half again from 1991 to 1992. Pretax and after-tax earnings both fell more than 80 percent from 1989 to 1992.

Net sales rose to record levels over the same period, so profit margins eroded faster than earnings. Operating earnings fell 72 percent, for example, while the operating margin fell 79 percent, from 14 cents on the

(for years ended December 31;
dollar amounts in millions)

1989	1990	1991	1992	
$11,378	$12,960	$12,703	$13,598	Net Sales
7,918	9,263	9,316	10,137	Cost of Products Sold
$ 3,460	$ 3,697	$ 3,387	$ 3,461	*Gross Profit on Sales* ....
				Operating Expenses:
$ 559	$ 667	$ 725	$ 850	Depreciation and amortization
411	528	569	629	Distribution expenses
789	934	945	981	Selling and administrative expenses
91	133	135	150	Taxes other than payroll and income taxes
	212	60	398	Unusual charges
$ 1,850	$ 2,474	$ 2,434	$ 3,008	Total Operating Expenses, excluding income taxes
$ 1,610	$ 1,223	$ 953	$ 453	*Earnings from Operations, before income taxes* ....
205	277	315	247	Interest Expense, net
				Earnings before Income Taxes, Extraordinary Item,
$ 1,405	$ 946	$ 638	$ 206	*and Cumulative Effect of Accounting Changes*
541	377	239	64	Provision for Income Taxes
				Earnings before Extraordinary Item
$ 864	$ 569	$ 399	$ 142	*and Cumulative Effect of Accounting Changes* ....
			(6)	Extraordinary Item — loss on extinguishment of debt
		(215)	(50)	Cumulative Effects of Accounting Changes
$ 864	$ 569	$ 184	$ 86	**Net Earnings** ....
19				Preferred Dividend Requirements
$ 845	$ 569	$ 184	$ 86	*Earnings Applicable to Common Shares*

Addenda

1989	1990	1991	1992	
$ 112	$ 179	$ 247	$ 232	Average Cash and Temporary Investments ....
803	1,014	1,102	1,185	Average Accounts Payable
6,615	7,520	8,315	9,117	Average Fixed Assets
10,522	12,626	14,305	15,700	Average Total Assets
1,337	1,675	1,893	2,035	Average Inventories (FIFO basis)
7,921	9,250	9,318	10,152	Cost of Products Sold (FIFO basis)
1,381	1,711	1,885	1,934	Average Gross Receivables
48	98	262	118	Principal Repayment Requirements

Short-Term Solvency Measures

1989	1990	1991	1992	
5.9	5.5	4.9	5.0	Average Inventory Turnover (FIFO basis)
62	66	74	73	Days to Sell Average Inventory
8.2	7.6	6.7	7.0	Average Receivables Turnover
44	48	54	52	Days to Collect Average Receivables
106	114	128	125	Operating Cycle (days)

Long-Term Solvency Measures

1989	1990	1991	1992	
7.9	4.4	3.0	1.8	Interest Coverage Ratio
6.4	3.3	1.7	1.2	Fixed Charges Ratio

Sources: *International Paper Annual Report for 1989, 1990, 1991,* and *1992* (Purchase, NY:
International Paper Company, 1990-93). The notes in each *Annual Report* are integral parts of the
original statements.

	As fractions of net sales* (common-size statements)				As percentages of 1989 levels (index numbers or trend percentages)			Annual percent changes		
	1989	1990	1991	1992	1990	1991	1992	1990	1991	1992
	1.00	1.00	1.00	1.00	114%	112%	120%	13.9%	−2.0%	7.0%
	0.70	0.71	0.73	0.75	117	118	128	17.0	0.6	8.8
······	0.30	0.29	0.27	0.25 ···	107	98	100 ······	6.8	−8.4	2.2
	0.05	0.05	0.06	0.06	119	130	152	19.3	8.7	17.2
	0.04	0.04	0.04	0.05	128	138	153	28.5	7.8	10.5
	0.07	0.07	0.07	0.07	118	120	124	18.4	1.2	3.8
	0.01	0.01	0.01	0.01	146	148	165	46.2	1.5	11.1
		0.02	0.00	0.03						
	0.16	0.19	0.19	0.22	134	132	163	33.7	−1.6	23.6
······	0.14	0.09	0.08	0.03 ···	76	59	28 ·····	−24.0	−22.1	−52.5
	0.02	0.02	0.02	0.02	135	154	120	35.1	13.7	−21.6
	0.12	0.07	0.05	0.02	67	45	15	−32.7	−32.6	−67.7
	0.05	0.03	0.02	0.00	70	44	12	−30.3	−36.6	−73.2
······	0.08	0.04	0.03	0.01 ···	66	46	16 ·····	−34.1	−29.9	−64.4
				(0.00)						
			(0.02)	(0.00)						
······	0.08	0.04	0.01	0.01 ···	66	21	10 ·····	−34.1	−67.7	−53.3
	0.00									
	0.07	0.04	0.01	0.01	67	22	10	−32.7	−67.7	−53.3

Turnover Ratios

······ 101.6	72.4	51.4	58.7	= net sales ÷ average cash and temporary investments
14.2	12.8	11.5	11.5	= net sales ÷ average accounts payable
1.7	1.7	1.5	1.5	= net sales ÷ average fixed assets
1.1	1.0	0.9	0.9	= net sales ÷ average total assets

average inventory turnover = cost of products sold ÷ average inventory

days to sell average inventory = 365 ÷ average inventory turnover

average receivables turnover = net sales ÷ average gross receivables

days to collect average receivables = 365 ÷ average receivables turnover

operating cycle (days) = days to sell avg. inventory + days to collect avg. receivables

interest coverage ratio = pretax operating earnings ÷ net interest expense

$$\text{fixed charges ratio} = \frac{\text{pretax operating earnings}}{\text{net interest expense + principal repayment requirements}}$$

* Detail items may not add up to totals because of round-off error.

INTERNATIONAL PAPER COMPANY
Sample Analysis of Income Statement
(continued)

(for years ended December 31)

1989	1990	1991	1992	**Selected Per-Share Measures***
$104.00	$118.68	$114.96	$112.01	Net Sales
72.38	84.83	84.31	83.50	Cost of Products Sold
$ 31.62	$ 33.85	$ 30.65	$ 28.51	*Gross Profit on Sales* · ◄
$ 5.11	$ 6.11	$ 6.56	$ 7.00	Depreciation and amortization
3.76	4.84	5.15	5.18	Distribution expenses
7.21	8.55	8.55	8.08	Selling and administrative expenses
0.83	1.22	1.22	1.24	Taxes other than payroll and income taxes
	1.94	0.54	3.28	Unusual charges
$ 16.91	$ 22.66	$ 22.02	$ 24.78	Total Operating Expenses, excluding income taxes
$ 14.71	$ 11.19	$ 8.63	$ 3.73	*Earnings from Operations, before income taxes* · · · · · · · · · · · · ◄
1.87	2.54	2.85	2.03	Interest Expense, net
4.95	3.45	2.16	0.53	Provision for Income Taxes
0.17				Preferred Dividend Requirements
				Earnings Applicable to Common Shares, before extraordinary item and cumulative effects
$ 7.72	$ 5.21	$ 3.61	$ 1.17	*of accounting changes* ·
			(0.05)	Extraordinary Item — loss on extinguishment of debt
		(1.95)	(0.41)	Cumulative Effects of Accounting Changes
$ 7.72	$ 5.21	$ 1.66	$ 0.71	**Earnings per Common Share** ·

Addenda

1989	1990	1991	1992	
$56.500	$53.500	$70.750	$66.625	Market Price per Common Share (year-end)
1.53	1.68	1.68	1.68	Dividends per Common Share
109.4	109.2	110.5	121.4	Weighted Average Common Shares Outstanding (millions) · · · · · ◄
7.3	10.3	19.6	56.9	Price-Earnings Ratio (recurring)
7.3	10.3	42.6	93.8	Price-Earnings Ratio (net)
(in millions)				
$4,852	$5,390	$5,686	$5,964	Average Common Shareholders' Equity
2,723	3,762	4,617	5,251	Average Borrowed Funds
10,522	12,626	14,305	15,700	Average Total Assets

Return on Investment Measures

1989	1990	1991	1992	
7.53%	7.36%	6.82%	4.70%	Average Effective Interest Rate
15.30	9.69	6.66	2.89	Return on Assets
17.42	10.56	3.24	1.44	Return on Equity
1.1	1.1	0.5	0.5	Financial Leverage Index
2.71%	3.14%	2.37%	2.52%	Dividend Yield
25.13	−2.34	35.38	−3.46	Total Return on Common Shares

* Detail items may not add up to totals because of round-off error.

As percentages of 1989 levels (index numbers or trend percentages)			Annual percent changes		
1990	1991	1992	1990	1991	1992
114	111	108	14.1	−3.1	−2.6
117	116	115	17.2	−0.6	−1.0
107	97	90	7.1	−9.5	−7.0
120	128	137	19.6	7.4	6.7
129	137	138	28.7	6.4	0.6
119	119	112	18.6	0.0	−5.5
147	147	149	47.0	0.0	1.6
134	130	147	34.0	−2.8	12.5
76	59	25	−23.9	−22.9	−56.8
136	152	109	35.8	12.2	−28.8
70	44	11	−30.3	−37.4	−75.5
67	47	15	−32.5	−30.7	−67.6
67	22	9	−32.5	−68.1	−57.2
95	125	118	−5.3	32.2	−5.8
110	110	110	9.8	0.0	0.0
100	101	111	−0.2	1.2	9.9
140	268	778	40.3	90.9	190.6
140	582	1282	40.3	315.1	120.2

average effective interest rate = net interest expense ÷ average borrowed funds
return on assets = pretax operating earnings ÷ average total assets
return on equity = earnings applicable to common shares ÷ average common equity

financial leverage index = return on equity ÷ return on assets

dividend yield = dividend per share ÷ market price per share
total return on common shares = dividend per share + change in market price
                                ───
                                         beginning market price

dollar to 3 cents. Unlike earnings, gross profits remained flat over the 4-year period, but as sales increased, the gross margin fell from 30 cents on the dollar to 25 cents.

The company's earnings and profit margins plunged for two reasons. First, the cost of products sold and all of the other operating expense items increased faster than sales. The increase in the cost of products sold from 70 percent of net sales in 1989 to 75 percent in 1992 was the most notable. The recurring operating expense items posted only marginal increases as percentages of net sales. The second reason for plunging earnings was the series of unusual charges, notably in 1990 and 1992. These charges accounted for more than a third of the growth in total operating expenses. In addition, the extraordinary after-tax charges in 1991 and 1992 contributed to the collapse of net earnings.

Ratio Analysis

Ratio analysis is a lot like cooking: like a chef, each analyst has a slightly different formula for computing a given ratio; like ingredients, the available disclosures determine what gets computed. The ratios that we present in the sample analysis are "standard fare," but the list is by no means comprehensive, nor should the formulas used be taken as gospel. Those who take the time to churn out some of the innumerable variations on these formulas will find that no one measure is reliable or useful all of the time — a thorough analysis is important. That said, number-crunching quickly becomes an exercise in diminishing returns.

Although seldom acknowledged as such, per-share measures are ratios. The denominator of any per-share ratio is the weighted average number of common shares outstanding. Earnings per common share is thus the most frequently encountered income-statement ratio.

Earnings per share provides a useful yardstick for evaluating a corporation's share price:

(1) $$\text{price-earnings ratio} = \frac{\text{market price per common share}}{\text{net earnings per common share}}$$

As explained in Chapter IV, many analysts compare share prices by computing the present values of corporations' projected earnings per share. The calculations involved are complex, but given certain assumptions about future earnings trends, comparisons of P-E ratios will give the same answers for much less work. Although the necessary assumptions rarely apply, the ease of computing P-E ratios has led to their widespread use.

It is impossible to evaluate in advance the accuracy of the many earnings projections that are available — predicting earnings is not yet a science. A common substitute for the forward-looking P-E ratio is the ratio based on the latest reported earnings. This substitute is the number that appears in the stock tables in the newspaper, and in the sample analysis in this chapter. When earnings are expected to grow, which is often, this retrospective P-E ratio does not reflect the rosy earnings expectations that form the basis for the current market price. For this reason, the calculation of the retrospective P-E ratio can be a useful exercise in conservatism.

If the latest earnings report is to be used as a conservative estimate of future earnings, it is important to exclude any extraordinary items:

$$\text{(2) price-earnings ratio} = \frac{\text{market price per share}}{\text{earnings per share before extraordinary items}}$$

By definition, extraordinary items are those that cannot reasonably be expected to recur, so any earnings projection, no matter how conservative, should exclude past extraordinary items.

| 7.3 | 10.3 | 19.6 | 56.9 Price-Earnings Ratio (recurring) |
| 7.3 | 10.3 | 42.6 | 93.8 Price-Earnings Ratio (net) |

For International Paper, this exclusion made the difference between outrageous and merely lofty in 1991 and 1992. Ratios in the neighborhood of 90 usually are reserved for biotechnology companies, purveyors of digital interactive services, and other speculative issues.

The usefulness of per-share measures other than earnings per share depends on the variability of the number of shares outstanding. The sample analysis includes a per-share restatement of most items on International Paper's income statement. The horizontal analysis that accompanies it reveals little difference between the per-share change and the unadjusted change in each item during 1990 and 1991. In 1992, however, the company issued a substantial number of new shares:

| 109.4 | 109.2 | 110.5 | 121.4 Weighted Average Common Shares Outstanding (millions) |

That transaction put the 1992 changes in the per-share items much lower than the corresponding changes in the unadjusted items. Although this difference was barely noticeable in the plunging measures of earnings — the plunges were slightly steeper on a per-share basis — it was more evident among the other line items. Several items posted modest increases in dollar terms but decreased on a per-share basis. One such item was net sales, which reached a record level in 1992, but only before adjustment for the stock offering.

The Operating Cycle and Short-Term Solvency

Chapter III presented the current ratio as a measure of short-term solvency. The current ratio is poorly suited for its assigned task because it does not account for time. A business's current assets might outweigh its current liabilities by the vaunted 2:1 margin, but the ratio is of little consequence if the liabilities are all due tomorrow and the assets are all raw materials inventories. That is an extreme example, of course, but solvency does depend on the composition of current assets and the timing of current liabilities. Accountants analyze asset composition in terms of quality, which is the likelihood of an asset's conversion to cash without any loss, and liquidity, which is the amount of time and effort the conversion will take. Two key measures of asset composition are inventory and receivables turnover, which measure the liquidity of those assets.

A turnover ratio expresses sales volume for a period as a multiple of the balance in an asset account. The asset balance usually is an average for the period, which can be calculated many ways. The most common method, especially with annual data, is to take the average of the beginning and ending balances for a period. Another common method of calculating an annual average, if quarterly data are available, is to take the average of the four end-of-quarter balances. The more change there is in an asset account, the more important it is to include several interim balances in the average.

Inventories are valued at cost, so an accurate inventory turnover ratio must value sales at cost too. The cost of products sold, rather than net sales, therefore is the appropriate denominator of the inventory turnover ratio:

(3) average inventory turnover = cost of products sold ÷ average inventory

As discussed in Chapter II, there are several ways to determine the cost of inventories. The LIFO method is the most common, given the prevailing conditions of price inflation, but it produces relatively low inventory valuations. These low valuations tend to exaggerate turnover, so it is important to use the FIFO method in inventory turnover ratios. Fortunately for the analyst, the notes to financial statements usually include an estimate of the amount by which inventories on a FIFO basis would differ from reported LIFO inventories, so adjusting reported inventories is simply a matter of addition. The necessary adjustment to the cost of products sold is not so obvious:

(4) FIFO cost of products sold = LIFO cost of products sold
  + FIFO adjustment to beginning inventory
  − FIFO adjustment to ending inventory

Turnover ratios typically use annual sales in the numerator, measuring the number of times a business must replenish its average stock of inventories in a year. An alternative way to evaluate the pace of sales is to measure the time it takes to sell the average stock:

(5) days to sell average inventory = 365 ÷ average inventory turnover

Many analysts consider this measure easier to interpret than the inventory turnover ratio.

By either measure, International Paper's sales slowed significantly in 1990 and 1991 and improved marginally in 1992. Inventory turnover fell from nearly six times per year to five times between 1989 and 1992, and it took an additional 11 days to sell the average inventory at the end of the 4 years. Although these developments clearly were unfavorable, increasing turnover is not always a good thing. Frequent stockouts and large order backlogs may interrupt production and drive away customers. A case in point is the recent disruption of production at General Motors due to inadequate parts inventories.

If the notes to the financial statements disclose the composition of inventories, the analyst should prepare a common-size breakdown of inventories to determine the relative proportions of raw materials, work in process, parts, and finished goods. If solvency is a concern, the proportion of finished goods in inventories can be critically important. In addition, sharp changes in the proportions of inventory components may provide early signs of production, purchasing, or sales difficulties.

Inventory turnover and days to sell inventories do not measure the liquidity of inventories directly, unless the business in question makes most of its sales for cash. The prevailing practice outside of the retail sector is to sell on credit, which gives rise to accounts and notes receivable. Receivables turnover and days to collect receivables are thus important measures of liquidity:

(6) average receivables turnover = net sales ÷ average gross receivables

(7) days to collect average receivables = 365 ÷ average receivables turnover

It is appropriate to use net sales in the turnover ratio, rather than the cost of sales, because businesses value receivables at the sales price of merchandise, not at cost. Similarly, the analyst should use gross receivables to compute turnover, not net receivables, because the allowance for uncollectible accounts reflects a reduction in quality rather than an increase in liquidity.

International Paper's experience with receivables collection closely tracked the company's inventory conversion record from 1989 to 1992: turnover slowed from 1989 to 1991 and improved slightly in 1992. It took 8 more days to collect average receivables in 1992 than it did in 1989. Low or declining receivables turnover is unfavorable, indicating slow sales or a weak collections effort. High receivables turnover has its own drawbacks; a business with high receivables turnover may be turning away sales by insisting on stringent credit terms. As with inventory turnover and other turnover ratios, a business must strike a balance between excessive caution and overtrading.

Businesses can boost turnover by discounting receivables. Discounting is the sale of receivables to third parties before maturity, usually for less than face value. This is an age-old business practice, but the recent trend toward the securitization of every conceivable form of credit has made it increasingly popular. If a business sells receivables with recourse, it continues to bear the risk of uncollectible accounts. Selling with recourse is a form of off-balance-sheet financing, and it overstates the receivables turnover ratio if the allowance for uncollectible accounts is inadequate. It is important to check for disclosure of this practice in the notes to a business's financial statements.

Days to sell inventory and days to collect receivables are informative measures by themselves, but it also is useful to consider them together:

(8)   operating cycle = days to sell average inventory
                              + days to collect average receivables

The length of a business's operating cycle determines its short-term financing needs and is a gauge of its solvency. In traditional financing arrangements, a business takes out short-term loans to buy inventories and then repays the loans from collections of receivables. When these arrangements prevail, the liabilities due during the next operating cycle should not exceed the average amounts of cash, receivables, and inventories, plus a margin of safety. As an analysis of solvency, a calculation of the length of the operating cycle is no substitute for a comparison of the exact amounts due and receivable 30, 60, and 90 days hence, but businesses seldom disclose such detailed information.

Turnover, Efficiency, and Flexibility

Turnover ratios are not limited to inventories and receivables, they can be computed for any asset, for groups of assets, and for some liabilities too. Above, we introduced inventory and receivables turnover as starting points for solvency analysis, but that application is unique to those two ratios. All turnover ratios measure how intensively businesses use their resources, including receivables and inventories.

Every turnover ratio involves a trade-off. With inventories, businesses must balance costly excess stocks, the symptom of low turnover, against shortages, production bottlenecks, and other perils of high turnover. With receivables, low turnover suggests inefficient collection efforts or poor credit screening; high turnover suggests sales lost due to tight credit. In general, the trade-off is between efficiency and flexibility.

Efficiency involves minimizing the cost of existing operations by maxi-

56

mizing the use of resources. An efficient business maintains or increases its earnings by keeping its profit margins high. In contrast, flexibility involves minimizing the cost of expanding operations by keeping resources in reserve. Often it is possible to expand operations by expanding the resource base, but usually it is cheaper to press into service the idle resources on hand. A flexible business boosts its earnings by increasing its volume of operations and its market share.

The analyst has hundreds of turnover ratios to choose from, given the variety of assets and liabilities and the many possible groupings in either category. The sample analysis of International Paper's income statement presents four of the most useful ratios (not counting inventory and receivables turnover), three for assets and one for liabilities. Net sales is the numerator of all four ratios. These four ratios all followed the same pattern as the company's inventory and receivables turnover, posting significant declines from 1989 to 1991 and leveling off or improving slightly in 1992. Asset and liability ratios take opposite interpretations: high turnover indicates an efficient, inflexible use of assets and a flexible, inefficient use of liabilities.

Cash turnover is important because cash is the lifeblood of business. A business with excessive cash turnover bears a significant risk of insolvency. The analyst should determine the adequacy of such a business's short-term credit facilities. Excessive cash balances, on the other hand, are a sign of inefficiency; there is no return on idle cash balances. There is a return on temporary investments, however, so a low turnover of cash and temporary investments is more efficient than an equally low turnover of cash alone.

Accounts payable turnover is important because trade credit is free, unlike other forms of credit, as long as it is paid promptly. Because the balance of accounts payable is closely related to the volume of sales, changes in this ratio are particularly important. When sales are rising, increasing turnover indicates that a business could be taking greater advantage of this source of free financing. When sales are falling, increasing turnover suggests a curtailment of trade credit, which could be disastrous. Decreasing accounts payable turnover indicates deterioration in a business's current position and an increasing risk of insolvency.

Fixed assets turnover and total assets turnover are broad measures of asset utilization. Both ratios emphasize the utilization of capital assets rather than current assets. Total asset turnover tends to be more useful for analyzing service businesses, which rely heavily on intellectual property and other intangibles, than for manufacturing businesses, for which fixed asset turnover is vital. These ratios can fluctuate widely because capital investment and corporate acquisitions produce large changes in assets.

Long-Term Solvency

Solvency is a business's ability to meet its cash obligations on time and in full. Short-term solvency therefore depends on the adequacy of cash flows. Over the long term, solvency includes an additional hurdle: a business must earn enough to maintain its financial and physical capital. When capital maintenance is inadequate, a business is reducing the scale of its operations, which tends to involve a gut-wrenching series of write-offs and reorganizations — and often bankruptcy — rather than an orderly liquidation process. These difficulties attending a failure to maintain capital can increase substantially the risk of short-term insolvency.

From the long-term creditor's point of view, it is a risky proposition to lend to a business that has a capital maintenance problem. Depreciation, write-offs, and other noncash expenses allow a financially sound business to build up cash reserves to meet its principal repayment requirements. When revenues are insufficient to cover noncash expenses, however, the risk that the business will default on its principal rises, because there is no opportunity to set aside the necessary cash. A business in this position can avoid default by refinancing its debt, but given the poor operating results, creditors will require higher interest payments to assume the increasing risk. This situation can develop into a vicious circle, in which increased interest payments put a burden on cash flows that erodes solvency even further, raising both the cost of future refinancing and the likelihood of default.

The interest coverage ratio is one of the most useful measures of long-term solvency:

$$(9) \qquad \text{interest coverage ratio} = \frac{\text{pretax operating earnings}}{\text{net interest expense}}$$

An interest coverage ratio greater than 1 indicates that a business's operating earnings exceed its interest expense, in which case a business has met all of its cash obligations (except for income taxes), and thereby has achieved short-term solvency. Having met its operating expenses, which include noncash allowances for capital maintenance, the business also has attained long-term solvency. It is appropriate to exclude income taxes from this calculation because interest and most operating expenses are tax-deductible, so taxes apply only when income remains after these deductions.

A quick way of determining a business's long-term solvency is to check whether pretax earnings are positive. If so, then the interest coverage ratio will be greater than 1. The drawback of this method is that there is no simple way to compare the pretax earnings of different businesses. The analyst can use pretax earnings to determine that two businesses are solvent, but only the interest coverage ratio will reveal which one enjoys a greater margin of solvency.

A conservative measure of long-term solvency is the fixed charges ratio. The phrase "fixed charges ratio" has generated more than the usual degree of inconsistent usage. Some analysts equate it with the interest coverage ratio. The SEC has published an extraordinarily complex formula for the ratio that it requires in official disclosures. The following formula is much simpler:

$$(10) \quad \begin{array}{c} \text{fixed} \\ \text{charges} \\ \text{ratio} \end{array} = \frac{\text{pretax operating earnings}}{\text{net interest expense} + \text{principal repayment requirements}}$$

This ratio is appropriate when the pattern or amount of a business's depreciation and other noncash charges differs markedly from that of its sinking-fund requirements and other principal repayments. This is most likely to be the case among businesses that borrow for purposes other than acquiring depreciable assets. The conservative bias applies to businesses that do use depreciation to accumulate cash reserves. Double counting occurs in these cases because principal repayment requirements appear in the denominator while depreciation, their proxy, is deducted from the numerator.

The judgments of the professional credit-rating services are important adjuncts to the analyst's own work, especially for the inexperienced analyst. The major rating services are Moody's Investors Service, Standard & Poor's Corporation, Fitch Investors Service, and Duff & Phelps. Most public libraries carry publications from one or more of these services. Each service has its own proprietary rating system, but they all are variations on the letter grades used in schools.

Judging by its pretax earnings, International Paper remained solvent from 1989 through 1992, but both the interest coverage and fixed charges ratios deteriorated sharply. Unlike the short-term solvency measures, the long-term measures continued to deteriorate during 1992, rather than leveling off. Although the company's financial capital increased during the period, as measured by the size of the balance sheet, the unusual charges for asset writedowns and layoffs in 1990, 1991, and 1992 suggest developing problems with the maintenance of physical capital and of the scale of operations. Despite these developments, Standard and Poor's *Bond Guide* for October 1993 rates International Paper's senior bonds at A⁻, the lower end of investment grade. Standard and Poor's has not changed its ratings of the company's senior debt since October 1986, when it downgraded them from A⁺ to A⁻.

59

Leverage and Return on Investment

Long-term solvency is the bondholder's paramount concern because it ensures an uninterrupted series of interest and principal payments. The bondholder's investment decision hinges almost exclusively on an assessment of risk, because the returns on bonds are essentially fixed. Up to a point, bondholders can demand higher interest payments for assuming unusual risks, but this strategy becomes self-defeating when debt service becomes so burdensome as to weaken a borrower's financial position.

The shareholder's investment decision is an assessment of risk *and* return. Shareholders' returns are uncertain, unlike bondholders,' so shareholders must determine whether a corporation can use borrowed funds effectively, rather than merely competently. Shareholders stand to gain much more than bondholders if a corporation uses leverage effectively. Long-term solvency is, of course, a major concern of shareholders, but it weighs relatively less in their investment decisions.

A key element of a business's effective use of leverage is the cost of borrowing, which the analyst should weigh against the benefits of borrowing, if possible. The income statement affords a rough measure of the cost of borrowing:

(11)   average effective interest rate = $\dfrac{\text{net interest expense}}{\text{average borrowed funds}}$

Borrowed funds in this equation consist of short-term notes payable and long-term debt, including current maturities. An exact measure of the effective interest rate would use the weighted average of borrowed funds outstanding, but that seldom is disclosed.

An interest rate acts as a hurdle rate of return for capital investment projects and corporate acquisitions to be financed by borrowing: investments expected to return less than the prospective interest rate do not "clear the hurdle" and should not be undertaken — the costs are likely to outweigh the benefits. Because businesses base investment decisions on prospective rates, the average effective interest rate is useful primarily for assessing projects already undertaken. When interest rates are relatively stable, however, the average effective rate can provide a reasonable forecast of prospective rates.

The cost of leverage is readily identifiable — it is interest expense, the return to bondholders — but the benefits of leverage are more difficult to measure. In most cases, it is impossible for equity owners to distinguish the extra returns attributable to leverage from the returns that a business could have provided without using leverage, given the same equity base. Even when businesses disclose to equity owners detailed accountings of the returns on each capital project and acquisition, which seldom happens, there is not necessarily an exact correspondence between borrowings and investments. For these reasons, the analyst must infer the benefits of leverage from measures of return on investment.

Return on investment quantifies a management's efficiency in employing the resources entrusted to it. Return-on-investment measures are ratios of returns to resources. There are a number of ways to count a business's returns and resources, so the scope of return-on-investment ratios can vary considerably. One of the broadest and most important ratios is return on assets:

(12) return on assets = pretax operating earnings ÷ average total assets

It includes every resource on the balance sheet, however financed, and the broadest measure of net returns. To be any broader, a return-on-investment ratio would have to include off-balance-sheet-financing items, such as operating leases and the debt of unconsolidated subsidiaries. A similar ratio using gross returns (*i.e.*, sales) in the numerator would be a turnover ratio. Turnover measures the intensity of the use of resources, whereas return on investment measures efficiency.

From the shareholder's point of view, return on equity is a key return-on-investment ratio:

$$(13) \quad \text{return on equity} = \frac{\text{earnings applicable to common shares}}{\text{average common shareholders' equity}}$$

This ratio is a more selective measure than return on assets. Whereas return on assets measures management's ability to earn a return using the assets at hand, return on equity measures management's ability to provide a return to shareholders using the available equity base.

Although disclosures and analyses commonly cite return on equity, it suffers from some serious drawbacks. First, the book value of common shareholders' equity often bears little relation to its market value, so that shares cannot be purchased at anything approaching book value. For corporations in this situation, return on equity is not a literal measure of returns to shareholders. Second, the book value of equity does not include tacit forms of equity, such as minority interest (for which market value also can differ markedly from book value) and deferred income tax liabilities.

Despite these drawbacks, return on equity is a useful ratio. One important use for the ratio is in evaluations of the effectiveness of leverage:

(14) financial leverage index = return on equity ÷ return on assets

Leverage enables a business to purchase a stock of assets larger than its

61

equity base. If those extra assets are more productive than the cost of borrowing, then return on equity exceeds return on assets and the financial leverage index exceeds 1. This is the desired result. If the financial leverage index equals 1, then leverage is a wash. If the index falls below 1, leverage is doing more harm than good.

The sample analysis of International Paper's income statement shows that the company used assets and leverage effectively as late as 1990, but that it experienced a dramatic loss of efficiency in 1991 and 1992. Return on assets and return on equity both plunged in those 2 years. The plunge illustrates how leverage can be a double-edged sword. Leverage boosted return on equity during the fat years: return on equity exceeded return on assets by 2 full percentage points during 1989, and the leverage index remained above 1 in 1990. On the other hand, leverage produced a disproportionate recessionary drop in return on equity, which was less than half of return on assets during 1991 and 1992.

Shareholder Returns

Return on equity indicates management's efficiency in providing a return to shareholders, but it is a poor measure of shareholder returns. Return on equity is enormously useful because it summarizes the flood of data that the GAAP framework makes possible. The problem with return on equity is the problem with GAAP: it accounts for only a portion of the transactions that affect corporate share prices. Changes in share prices constitute the bulk of shareholder returns, so it is GAAP's failure to account for these changes that makes return on equity such a poor measure of shareholder returns.

Accounting data measure the past transactions of a corporation, but the price of its shares depends on investors' expectations about the corporation's future transactions. Changes in earnings expectations play a particularly large role in determining share prices. In addition, there are many transactions that a corporation does *not* make that can affect its share price, such as those that change interest rates and other economic conditions, and those that change the prices of other corporations' shares.

Together with share-price changes, dividends are a major component of shareholder returns. Dividends are significant because they are much more reliable than share-price increases; they usually are paid on an announced schedule, and usually in cash. By contrast, capital gains come and go with the vagaries of the stock market, and they can be converted to cash only once. The reliability of dividends makes dividend yield a useful measure of shareholder returns:

(15)   dividend yield = dividend per share ÷ market price per share

By adjusting corporations' dividends for their share prices, this ratio affords direct comparisons of the payouts of different corporations.

A corporation's dividend yield is readily comparable to the percent change in its share price because both are expressed in percentage terms. The sum of these two measures gives (with some rearrangement):

$$(16) \quad \frac{\text{total return}}{\text{on common shares}} = \frac{\text{dividend per share} + \text{change in market price}}{\text{beginning market price}}$$

This formula applies only when there are no extras, which include spin-offs, warrants, rights, stock dividends, and other noncash distributions to shareholders. If applicable, the cash value of extras should be added to the numerator of Equation (16). Total return is the bottom line from the shareholder's point of view. It is a comprehensive measure of the factors affecting a shareholder's investment experience, from management performance to investor sentiment.

INTERNATIONAL PAPER COMPANY

Consolidated Statement of Cash Flows (Indirect Method)
For the Year Ended December 31, 1992

Operating Activities	(in millions)
Net Earnings	$ 86
Cumulative Effect of Accounting Changes	50
Noncash Items:	
Productivity improvement charge	398
Depreciation and amortization	850
Deferred income taxes	(99)
Other, net	(95)
Changes in Current Assets and Liabilities:	
Accounts and notes receivable	2
Inventories	(127)
Accounts payable and accrued liabilities	(2)
Other	15
Cash Provided by Operations	**$1,078**

Investment Activities	
Invested in Capital Projects	($1,368)
Mergers and Acquisitions:	
Plants, properties, and equipment	(163)
Goodwill	(13)
Other assets and liabilities, net	23
Investments in Affiliated Companies	(247)
Other Investment	(104)
Cash Used for Investment Activities	**($1,872)**

Financing Activities	
Issuance of Common Stock	$ 703
Issuance of Debt	1,852
Reduction of Debt	(1,458)
Dividends Paid	(206)
Other Financing	(102)
Cash Provided by Financing Activities	**$ 789**
Effect of Exchange Rate Changes on Cash	($8)
Change in Cash and Temporary Investments	($13)
Cash and Temporary Investments:	
Beginning of year	238
End of year	$ 225

Adapted from *International Paper Annual Report for 1992* (Purchase, NY: International Paper Company, 1993), p. 44. The notes on pp. 46-52 of the *Annual Report* are an integral part of the original statement.

VI.

THE CASH FLOW STATEMENT

Ah, take the cash, and let the credit go,
Nor heed the rumble of a distant drum!

– The Rubaiyat of Omar Khayyam

A cash flow statement reconciles an enterprise's beginning and ending cash balances for a given accounting period by listing the various sources and uses of cash. The total of those items is the net change in cash, the difference between the beginning and ending balances. The cash flow statement is a close cousin of the familiar bank statement. Synonyms for the statement of cash flows include statement of changes in financial position, funds statement, and statement of sources and applications of funds, or "source & app" for short. Since 1987, the FASB has required published statements to use "Statement of Cash Flows" or a similar title, but the other names persist in conversation.

The cash flow statement resembles and complements the income statement. The income statement applies accrual accounting data to measure profitability. It does so by accounting for the change in retained earnings (except for the portion due to transactions with owners). The cash flow statement measures solvency by applying cash-basis accounting data to account for the change in cash. The cash flow statement is inappropriate for measuring profitability because the provision for capital maintenance, a necessary element of any measure of profitability, is a noncash item. Similarly, the income statement can only hint at solvency, because accrual accounting does not distinguish between cash and noncash revenues and expenses.

As the example at left shows, an important function of the cash flow statement is to classify cash flows into three broad categories: operating, investing, and financing activities. This classification reveals a business's ability to finance expansion internally and its reliance on outside financing. Ideally, a business should generate large cash inflows from operations, augment them with the leverage of cash inflows from financing, and, after providing for sufficient cash reserves, it should expand its operations *via* cash outflows for investing. Given the imperfect circumstances that prevail in practice, the appropriate course of action rarely is so clear.

Cash Flows from Operations

Operating cash flows are the flows that a business generates to produce net income. This classification reveals an important difference between the cash flow statement and the income statement: interest and income taxes

HOMEOWNERS GROUP, INC.

Consolidated Statement of Cash Flows (Direct Method)
For the Year Ended December 31, 1990

Cash Flows from Operating Activities:

Cash received from member and other fees	$19,818,321
Cash paid to members and others	(9,834,132)
Cash received from home warranty contracts	28,444,945
Cash paid for home warranty contract costs	(23,844,555)
Cash received for errors and omissions insurance	22,014,436
Cash paid for errors and omissions insurance	(22,246,858)
Cash paid to suppliers and employees	(8,834,215)
Cash received for dividends and interest	2,104,400
Cash paid for interest	(30,757)
Cash received from others	62,792
Cash paid for income taxes	(1,442,972)
Net Cash Provided by Operating Activities	**$ 6,211,405**

Cash Flows from Investing Activities:

Property and equipment expenditures, net	($ 734,901)
Payments for investments	(15,484,719)
Cost of investments sold	16,801,184
California member acquisition costs	(834,495)
Deferred new products implementation costs	8,359
Other	(117,725)
Net Cash Used in Investing Activities	**($ 362,297)**

Cash Flows from Financing Activities:

Net repayments of notes	($ 238,984)
Dividends paid on common stock	(596,225)
Purchase of treasury stock	(2,177,842)
Net Cash Used in Financing Activities	**($ 3,013,051)**

Net Increase in Cash	$ 2,836,057
Cash at Beginning of Year	1,377,858
Cash at End of Year	$ 4,213,915

Adapted from *Homeowners Group 1990 Annual Report* (Hollywood, FL: Homeowners Group Inc., 1991), p. 14. The notes on pp. 16-19 of the *Annual Report* are an integral part of the original statement.

are operating items on the cash flow statement, but not on the income statement. The difference arises because *net* income, and therefore operating cash flows, includes deductions for interest and taxes, but *operating* income does not.

There are two ways to measure operating cash flows: the direct method and the indirect method. Using the direct method, as shown at left, a business lists cash inflows and outflows from operations and their total, which is net cash flow from operations. The FASB encourages businesses to use the direct method, but it is rare for a business to do so, apparently because of the complexity of restating accrual-basis accounting records on a cash basis. We combed through four file drawers full of financial statements before we found the example at left.

The indirect method involves removing the accruals from net income. Beginning with net income, a business adds back noncash expenses and subtracts noncash revenues:

Net Earnings	$ 86
Cumulative Effect of Accounting Changes	50
Noncash Items:	
Productivity improvement charge	398
Depreciation and amortization	850
Deferred income taxes	(99)
Other, net	(95)

It then adds the increases in certain current liabilities and subtracts the increases in certain noncash current assets to arrive at net cash flow from operations:

Changes in Current Assets and Liabilities:	
Accounts and notes receivable	2
Inventories	(127)
Accounts payable and accrued liabilities	(2)
Other	15
Cash Provided by Operations	**$1,078**

This calculation excludes the changes in dividends payable, notes payable, and the current portion of long-term debt, and on the assets side, changes in loans receivable from officers. The remaining current items comprise operating working capital. The changes in current assets and liabilities appearing in the cash flow statement reflect the net change in operating working capital, except for the change in cash. The calculation of operating cash flows also excludes changes in noncurrent assets and liabilities, because only investing and financing activities involve cash transactions that produce changes in those accounts.

From the reader's point of view, the direct method is better than the indirect method. First, the FASB requires businesses that use the direct method to present as a supplementary disclosure the indirect method's reconciliation of net income and operating cash flows. Second, the indirect method reveals little about a business's operations that does not also appear on the income statement or the balance sheet. Third, like the income statement, the direct-method cash flow statement reveals the composition of a business's revenues and expenses, but on a cash basis rather than an accrual basis, thus providing additional useful information.

Cash Flows from Investing and Financing

The use of the indirect method is an option only for presenting cash flows from operations. Businesses must use the direct method to present cash flows from investing and cash flows from financing; there are no accrual-basis measures of these activities to restate on a cash basis.

Investing activities are transactions that affect noncurrent asset accounts, specifically fixed assets and investments in subsidiaries and in other affiliates. Cash flows from investing arise from capital investment projects, sales of fixed assets, mergers and acquisitions, divestitures, purchases and sales of securities, loans, and a variety of similar transactions:

Invested in Capital Projects	($1,368)
Mergers and Acquisitions:	
Plants, properties, and equipment	(163)
Goodwill	(13)
Other assets and liabilities, net	23
Investments in Affiliated Companies	(247)
Other Investment	(104)
Cash Used for Investment Activities	**($1,872)**

Investment is a vital business activity because depreciation is inevitable. Given the current rapid advances in technology, businesses must contend with obsolescence as a source of depreciation in addition to traditional wear and tear. A business that does not invest enough to compensate for depreciation is shrinking its capital base and the scale of its operations. As described on page 58, such shrinkage seldom is an orderly process.

Financing is a vital source of cash for businesses that require a level of investment greater than cash flows from operations. This situation is typical of young, developing businesses and of companies intent on rapid expansion. Financing activities include most transactions that affect equity and long-term liabilities, including the current portion of long-term debt. A major exception to this classification is that operating activities affect retained earnings by producing net income. Cash flows from financing arise from long-term borrowings and repayments, issues of stock, purchases and sales of treasury stock, payments of dividends, and other related transactions:

Issuance of Common Stock	$ 703
Issuance of Debt	1,852
Reduction of Debt	(1,458)
Dividends Paid	(206)
Other Financing	(102)
Cash Provided by Financing Activities ·	**$ 789**

The statement of cash flows classifies dividend payments as financing transactions, but it classifies interest payments as operating transactions. This classification is counterintuitive because interest arguably is a financing item. By the definition above, however, financing activities must affect long-term liabilities or equity. Interest payments do not affect either, so they are not financing activities. Interest also is one of the items in the computation of net income, which makes it an operating cash flow.

Certain investing and financing transactions require no cash flows. Important examples of such transactions include purchases and sales of fixed assets in exchange for mortgages; mergers, acquisitions, and investments involving debt-equity swaps and exchanges of equity; and conversions of convertible securities to common stock. The statement of cash flows must include a separate schedule of these noncash transactions, if they are material.

The effect of exchange-rate changes on cash discloses the change between balance-sheet dates in the dollar value of cash balances denominated in foreign currencies. Exchange-rate changes are not strictly cash flows, but they appear in the statement of cash flows because they are necessary for reconciling the change in cash balances. Businesses subject to exchange-rate changes list this item separately from operating, investing, and financing activities because exchange-rate changes do not reflect a business's own transactions.

VII.

ANALYSIS OF THE CASH FLOW STATEMENT

M OST nonprofessionals throw away annual reports well before reaching the statement of cash flows. In contrast to the widespread familiarity of the income statement and the balance sheet, the cash flow statement remains somewhat obscure, even among financial professionals. One reason for this obscurity is that GAAP did not require businesses to prepare cash flow statements until 1971. The relative lack of exposure, however, is no indication of this statement's usefulness. Those who take the time to understand and analyze a business's cash flows will gain a valuable perspective on its solvency, the quality of its earnings, its reliance on outside financing, and the adequacy of its cash flows for maintaining and expanding operations.

A useful analysis of these topics requires some rearrangement of the cash flow statement, as the sample analysis on the following pages shows.* Published cash flow statements follow a 3-part format, which breaks out cash flows from operating, investing, and financing activities. This 3-part format is the result of the FASB's *Statement of Financial Accounting Standards* 95, published in 1987. Before SFAS 95, the customary format was a 2-part breakdown of the sources and uses of cash, including subtotals for operating and investing activities. This 2-part format allows for a proper common-size analysis, so we have recast International Paper's cash flow statement in two parts in the sample analysis. To retain all the useful information from the 3-part format, the sample analysis presents net financing cash flows as an addendum.

Earnings Quality and Operating Cash Flows

Accrual accounting affords managers substantial discretion. If they are so inclined, managers can use this discretion to obfuscate performance and manipulate earnings estimates by using "shoehorn accounting," the practice of structuring questionable transactions to fit the letter of GAAP, but not its spirit. The majority of businesses do not bend the rules, of course, but when interests conflict, as owners' and managers' interests often do, reasonable men will disagree about legitimate exercises of discretion. An analysis of the sources of cash, particularly operating cash flows, provides outsiders with an independent perspective on a business's affairs, one that management can only manipulate fraudulently. This independent perspective acts as a check against management's exercises in spin control, and against more serious abuses of discretion.

---

* Having a photocopy of these two pages at hand will make the discussion of the sample analysis easier to follow.

INTERNATIONAL PAPER COMPANY
Sample Analysis of Cash Flow Statement

(in millions, except as noted, at December 31)

1989	1990	1991	1992	Sources of Cash
$ 864	$ 569	$ 184	$ 86	Net Earnings
		215	50	Cumulative Effects of Accounting Changes
				Noncash Items:
	$ 212	$ 60	$ 398	Unusual charges
$ 559	667	725	850	Depreciation and amortization
96	38	30	(99)	Deferred income taxes
7	20	45	(95)	Other, net
$ 662	$ 937	$ 860	$1,054	Total Noncash Items ·
				Changes in Working Capital Items:
$ 5	($ 59)	$ 79	$ 2	Accounts and notes receivable
(154)	(55)	(74)	(127)	Inventories
72	(9)	(122)	(2)	Accounts payable and accrued liabilities
(2)	2	35	15	Other
($ 79)	($ 121)	($ 82)	($ 112)	Net Decrease (Increase) in Working Capital Items
$1,447	$1,385	$1,177	$1,078	Cash Provided by Operations ·
$ 33	$ 40	$ 45	$ 703	Issuance of Common Stock
1,729	967	1,583	1,852	Issuance of Debt
(843)	(634)	(589)	(1,458)	Reduction of Debt
$ 919	$ 373	$1,039	$1,097	Cash Provided by Financing Items
$2,366	$1,758	$2,216	$2,175	Total Sources of Cash ·
				Uses of Cash
$ 887	$1,267	$1,197	$1,368	Capital investment projects
452	142	131	163	Mergers and acquisitions
$1,339	$1,409	$1,328	$1,531	Total Fixed Assets Spending ·
108	81	211	13	Goodwill
(153)	(76)	115	(23)	Other assets and liabilities, net
361		258	247	Investments in Affiliated Companies
27	(3)	56	104	Other Investment
$1,682	$1,411	$1,968	$1,872	Cash Used for Investment Activities · · · · · · · · · · · · · · · · · ·
$ 165				Repurchase of Common Stock
320				Redemption of Preferred Stock
187	$ 183	$ 186	$ 206	Dividends Paid
35	27	76	102	Other Financing
$ 707	$ 210	$ 262	$ 308	Cash Used for Financing Items
$2,389	$1,621	$2,230	$2,180	Total Uses of Cash ·
(3)	(17)	4	8	Effect of Exchange Rate Changes on Cash
(20)	154	(18)	(13)	Change in Cash and Temporary Investments
				Addenda
$ 212	$ 163	$ 777	$ 789	Net Cash Provided by Financing Activities · · · · · · · · · · · · · ·
11,943	13,906	15,681	16,949	Average Investment in Assets
2,064	2,048	1,809	1,571	Adjusted Operating Cash Flow
11,378	12,960	12,703	13,598	Net Sales
$13.23	$12.68	$10.65	$8.88	Cash Flow per Share
1.7	2.4	6.4	12.5	Earnings Quality Ratio
0.49	0.66	0.37	0.79	Debt Refinancing Ratio
12.72%	10.69%	9.27%	7.93%	Cash Operating Margin
17.28	14.73	11.54	9.27	Cash Return on Assets

Adapted from *International Paper Annual Report for 1989, 1990, 1991* and *1992* (Purchase, NY: International Paper Company, 1990-93). The notes in each *Annual Report* are integral parts of the original statements.

	As fractions of total sources* (common-size statements)			As percentages of 1989 levels (index numbers or trend percentages)			Annual percent changes		
	1989	1990	1991	1992	1990	1991	1992	1990	1991	1992
	0.37	0.32	0.08	0.04	66%	21%	10%	−34.1%	−67.7%	−53.3%
			0.10	0.02						
		0.12	0.03	0.18						
	0.24	0.38	0.33	0.39	119	130	152	19.3	8.7	17.2
	0.04	0.02	0.01	(0.05)	40	31	(103)			
	0.00	0.01	0.02	(0.04)						
· · · · · · ·	0.28	0.53	0.39	0.48 · · · ·	142	130	159 · · · · ·	41.5	−8.2	22.6
	0.00	(0.03)	0.04	0.00						
	(0.07)	(0.03)	(0.03)	(0.06)	36	48	82	−64.3	34.5	71.6
	0.03	(0.01)	(0.06)	(0.00)	(13)	(169)	(3)			
	(0.00)	0.00	0.02	0.01						
	(0.03)	(0.07)	(0.04)	(0.05)	153	104	142	53.2	−32.2	36.6
· · · · · · ·	0.61	0.79	0.53	0.50 · · · · ·	96	81	74 · · · · · ·	−4.3	−15.0	−8.4
	0.01	0.02	0.02	0.32						
	0.73	0.55	0.71	0.85	56	92	107	−44.1	63.7	17.0
	(0.36)	(0.36)	(0.27)	(0.67)	75	70	173	−24.8	−7.1	147.5
	0.39	0.21	0.47	0.50	41	113	119	−59.4	178.6	5.6
· · · · · · ·	1.00	1.00	1.00	1.00 · · · ·	74	94	92 · · · ·	−25.7	26.1	−1.9
	0.37	0.72	0.54	0.63	143	135	154	42.8	−5.5	14.3
	0.19	0.08	0.06	0.07	31	29	36	−68.6	−7.7	24.4
· · · · · · ·	0.57	0.80	0.60	0.70 · · · ·	105	99	114 · · · · · ·	5.2	−5.7	15.3
	0.05	0.05	0.10	0.01	75	195	12	−25.0	160.5	−93.8
	(0.06)	(0.04)	0.05	(0.01)	50	(75)	15			
	0.15		0.12	0.11						
	0.01	(0.00)	0.03	0.05						
· · · · · · ·	0.71	0.80	0.89	0.86 · · · · ·	84	117	111 · · · ·	−16.1	39.5	−4.9
	0.07									
	0.14									
	0.08	0.10	0.08	0.09	98	99	110	−2.1	1.6	10.8
	0.01	0.02	0.03	0.05	77	217	291	−22.9	181.5	34.2
	0.30	0.12	0.12	0.14	30	37	44	−70.3	24.8	17.6
· · · · · · ·	1.01	0.92	1.01	1.00 · · · ·	68	93	91 · · · ·	−32.1	37.6	−2.2
	(0.00)	(0.01)	0.00	0.00						
	(0.01)	0.09	(0.01)	(0.01)						
· · · · · · ·	0.09	0.09	0.35	0.36 · · · · ·	77	367	372 · · · ·	−23.1	376.7	1.5

investment in assets = total assets + accumulated depreciation − current operating liabilities
adjusted cash flow = cash provided by operations + income tax payments + interest payments

cash flow per share = cash provided by operations + weighted average shares outstanding
earnings quality ratio = cash provided by operations + net earnings
debt refinancing ratio = reduction of debt + issuance of debt
cash operating margin = cash provided by operations + net sales
cash return on assets = adjusted operating cash flow + average investment in assets

*Detail items may not add up to totals because of round-off error.

For most businesses, the three most important sources of cash are net earnings, depreciation, and financing items. Net earnings and depreciation also account for the bulk of most businesses' operating cash flows. The common-size statements in the sample analysis reveal that International Paper fit this pattern during 1989 and 1990, but that its net earnings plunged in 1991 and 1992 due to a combination of unusual charges and accounting changes. The unusual charge was a substantial source of cash during 1990, and the sum of unusual charges and accounting changes provided more cash than net earnings did in 1991 and 1992. As a result of these developments, cash provided by operations fell only 26 percent between 1989 and 1992, while net earnings dropped 90 percent.

As the checklist on page 3 notes, unusual accounting practices that require further scrutiny (those that may be distorting earnings) are likely to show up in the section on noncash items in the sources of cash. Noncash amounts are easier for managers to manipulate than are cash amounts because the amounts of noncash items often depend on management's own estimates rather than on verifiable transactions. In contrast, cash items all involve transactions, which generate paper trails. It generally takes fraudu-lent acts to manipulate line items generated by transactions.

Managers who wish to put a positive spin on earnings have two ways to do so: they can exaggerate noncash additions to earnings (deductions from operating cash flows) and they can understate noncash deductions (additions to operating cash flows). Noncash additions to earnings are of greater concern to the analyst than understated noncash deductions, because a deduction, however much it is understated, is still a deduction. It does not have the potential to boost reported earnings above operating cash flows, whereas noncash additions do. The quality of earnings is highly suspect when net earnings exceed operating cash flows.

In one case of exaggerated earnings, a company recorded a write-off of fixed assets as a current asset, thus deferring the write-off expense. The company used its plans to sell the fixed assets to justify its unusual accounting. On the cash flow statement, this maneuver understated the amount of write-offs and overstated the increase in operating working capital, *but it had no effect on net cash flows*, which illustrates the value of the independent perspective that the cash flow statement provides.

International Paper's cash flow statements reveal no such manipulations of the noncash items. First, there was no shortage of charges against income during the 1990-92 period. Second, the additions to income, which appeared only in 1992, amounted to relatively small fractions of total noncash items, operating cash flows, and sources of cash. Third, the $99 million deferred income-tax credit would not have occurred in the absence

74

of the $398 million unusual charge. The only curious item is the $95 million credit for "Other, net." The notes to the financial statements do not disclose the composition of this item, nor why it fell so sharply during 1992.

Overall, International Paper has no problems with earnings quality, as measured by the earnings quality ratio:

(1) earnings quality ratio = cash provided by operations ÷ net earnings

When either net earnings or operating cash flows are negative, the analyst should use the difference between the two to measure earnings quality, because interpretation problems arise when negative numbers enter into the ratio. A ratio of 1.0 indicates that a business produced a dollar of operating cash flows for every dollar of earnings. For a given level of earnings, a higher ratio is more favorable. Rising earnings quality is not so favorable, however, if it reflects falling earnings *quantity*. This situation has plagued International Paper:

1.7   2.4   6.4   12.5 Earnings Quality Ratio

A ratio below 1.0 indicates highly unfavorable circumstances that the analyst should examine carefully. The reason to be concerned about low earnings quality is that a business cannot use net income to pay dividends, invest in plant and equipment, or repay loans; it must have cash.

When there is a substantial gap between earnings and cash flows, whether due to low earnings quality or, conversely, to low earnings, it is useful to compare the traditional accrual-basis measures of profitability with their cash-basis counterparts:

(2) cash flow per share = $\dfrac{\text{cash provided by operations}}{\text{weighted average common shares outstanding}}$

(3) cash operating margin = cash provided by operations ÷ net sales

(4) cash return on assets = $\dfrac{\text{adjusted operating cash flow}}{\text{average investment in assets}}$

These ratios do not measure profitability, of course, because cash flows do not account for depreciation, but the ratios do gauge the efficiency of a business's operations. Noncash items, which often account for much of the gap between earnings and cash flows, tend to distort measures of efficiency.

Cash flow per share complements earnings per share. Arguably, preferred dividend requirements should be deducted from the numerator to obtain cash flows applicable to common shares, but that measure has less

75

analytical significance than earnings applicable to common shares. In the example at hand the difference is immaterial:

| $13.23 | $12.68 | $10.65 | $8.88 | Cash Flow per Share |
| $ 7.72 | $ 5.21 | $ 1.66 | $0.71 | Earnings per Common Share |

The cash operating margin complements the net profit margin.

| 12.72% | 10.69% | 9.27% | 7.93% | Cash Operating Margin |
| 7.59 | 4.39 | 1.45 | 0.63 | Net Profit Margin |

The analyst also can use adjusted operating cash flow (operating cash flows before deducting cash payments for income taxes and interest) in the numerator to obtain a cash-basis ratio comparable to the gross profit margin. As a counterpart to operating profits, adjusted operating cash flow also serves as the numerator of cash return on assets.*

| 17.28 | 14.73 | 11.54 | 9.27 | Cash Return on Assets |
| 15.30 | 9.69 | 6.66 | 2.89 | Accrual Return on Assets |

The foregoing comparisons show that the 1989-92 decline in the efficiency of International Paper's operations, although drastic, was not as severe as the 90 percent drop in profitability suggests. The cash-basis ratios "only" fell between 30 and 50 percent, and operating cash flows only fell 26 percent. In the converse situation, in which earnings quality is low, the profitability measures would exceed and grow faster than the comparable efficiency measures.

Solvency and Financing Cash Flows

Strictly speaking, an enterprise is either solvent or insolvent; either it can meet its obligations promptly and in full or it cannot. When financial markets were less developed and when bankruptcy laws were stricter, determining insolvency was a simpler matter. Today, businesses can draw on cash flows from financing activities practically indefinitely. Healthy companies can roll over long-term debt indefinitely, or retire it by issuing stock. Such companies can draw on standby lines of credit to weather unexpected or seasonal cash squeezes. Troubled companies become takeover targets and issue rafts of junk bonds. If the takeover plans turn sour, banks step in to issue bridge loans. If the hoped-for turnaround is slow to arrive, companies can pay off the junk-bond holders and other creditors with stock, as long as enough cash remains to pay the bankruptcy lawyers. In short, solvency is a matter of degree.

---

* The main difference between the average investment in assets, the denominator of cash return on assets, and average total assets, the denominator of the accrual-basis ratio, is that the average investment counts fixed assets gross of depreciation. A minor difference is that the investment in assets counts operating working capital rather than total current assets. Although complex, these adjustments ensure comparability.

In this environment, a key measure of solvency is the relative proportion of financing items in the total sources of cash:

Cash Provided by Operations	0.61	0.79	0.53	0.50
Issuance of Common Stock	0.01	0.02	0.02	0.32
Issuance of Debt	0.73	0.55	0.71	0.85
Reduction of Debt	(0.36)	(0.36)	(0.27)	(0.67)
Cash Provided by Financing Items	0.39	0.21	0.47	0.50

In addition to this breakdown, it is important to assess the net issuance of debt:

Issuance of Debt	0.73	0.55	0.71	0.85
Less: Reduction of Debt	(0.36)	(0.36)	(0.27)	(0.67)
Net Issuance of Debt	0.37	0.19	0.44	0.18

The debt refinancing ratio also measures this relationship:

(5)   debt refinancing ratio = reduction of debt ÷ issuance of debt

The cash flow statement makes no distinction between short-term and long-term debt. This classification precludes an analysis of prepayments of long-term debt, but International Paper's 1992 income statement reports a $9 million pretax loss on extinguishment of debt, which suggests that the sharp increase in the debt refinancing ratio in 1992 is overstated.

As a business relies increasingly on financing items to provide cash, it becomes a riskier investment. If it borrows more, debt service will place mounting demands on operating cash flows. Creditors face the risk that the business will be unable to employ the proceeds of borrowing profitably enough to meet those demands. If not, equity owners risk a dilution of their interests, because the business will have to grant creditors an equity interest or it will have to raise additional equity capital, or even sell assets, to pay off creditors in cash.

A business need not be in default to turn to equity as a source of cash. International Paper is a case in point: the notes to the company's financial statements reveal that it used the proceeds of a $650 million stock offering in 1992 to pay down debt. Issuance of common stock, which was a negligible source of cash in the previous 3 years, accounted for 32 percent of cash sources in 1992. In hindsight, International Paper's use of leverage was ineffective: the leverage produced record sales and increasing stocks of assets, but profitability plunged and operating cash flows declined as the company failed to contain costs.

As this case makes clear, rapid growth of sales and assets is no guarantee of increasing solvency or profitability. A company can grow right out of business if it does not keep costs under control. Ideally, a company should use leverage to purchase an increasing stock of assets, which in turn should produce a rising volume of sales. Once a company has set this growth in motion, the sales increases should produce growing cash flows from operations to finance the continued expansion of the asset base, which in turn should support further increases in sales. Without adequate cost controls, however, the growth of operating cash flows will not match the growth of sales. Rather than risk a loss of market share by putting a halt to expansion, most companies faced with this situation will seek additional outside financing to support the continued expansion of their balance sheets.

Cash Flow Adequacy

As the foregoing discussion suggests, a business's operations must generate cash receipts adequate to fund certain key expenditures if the business is to avoid excessive reliance on outside financing, and the trend toward insolvency that accompanies it. First, to avoid outright insolvency, a business's operating cash receipts must satisfy all of its obligations to suppliers and employees, and its interest obligation to creditors. Operating cash receipts need only meet interest payments because refinancing is a legitimate source of cash for principal repayment. Second, operating cash receipts should provide for the maintenance of the existing stock of fixed assets. Third, if sales are rising, operating receipts should finance the necessary additions to the stock of working capital.

A business should consider paying a dividend only if its receipts from operations suffice to meet these three key expenditures. If not, a dividend would be either a redistribution from creditors to equity owners or a return *of* capital, but not a return on capital. This dividend policy is not a universal dictum, however. One notable exception is that a subsidiary's dividend payments are likely to reflect its parent's cash needs, notwithstanding any disinvestment concerns. In addition, steady and rising dividend payments are an important device for attracting investors. Most companies resist cutting dividends unless cash shortfalls threaten to persist for some time.

Free cash flow is the name that many analysts apply to the amount of operating receipts remaining after a business has provided for the hierarchy of expenditures outlined above. That said, no single definition of free cash flow has gained widespread acceptance, although the name itself is widely used. "Free" refers to management's discretion in using free cash flow to expand productive capacity, to invest in other companies, or to clean up the balance sheet by retiring debt and equity.

One reason for the lack of agreement about what constitutes free cash flow is that cash-basis accounting makes no distinction between capital maintenance and the expansion of productive capacity. Absent this distinction, analysts muddle through using a variety of approximations to the

78

idealized measure described above. One such approximation is the following formula, applied in the analysis of cash flow adequacy on pages 80-81:

(6)   free cash flow = cash provided by operations
                                 – fixed assets spending
                                 – dividends

Because the indirect method of computing operating cash flows is so prevalent, it generally is impractical to use gross cash receipts from operations as a starting point for the analysis.

Another common simplification is to substitute inventory additions for the increase in operating working capital. The rationale for this simplification is that increases in receivables tend to be self-financing, because they produce comparable increases in accounts payable and in certain accruals. International Paper's experience shows this to be a rough approximation, at best:

				Changes in Working Capital Items:
$ 5	($ 59)	$ 79	$ 2	Accounts and notes receivable
(154)	(55)	(74)	(127)	Inventories
72	(9)	(122)	(2)	Accounts payable and accrued liabilities

Because the analysis of cash flow adequacy begins with operating cash flows, inventory additions must be added back and then subtracted again, after fixed assets spending. For the sake of simplicity, Equation (6) excludes inventory additions altogether. Inventory reductions should be excluded from an analysis of adequacy when they occur.

As a dollar amount, free cash flow is not conducive to comparisons among companies, or to industry averages. The cash flow adequacy ratio, which falls below 1.00 when free cash flow is negative, allows for such comparisons:

(7) cash flow adequacy ratio =

$$\frac{\text{cash provided by operations + inventory additions}}{\text{fixed assets spending + inventory additions + dividends}}$$

International Paper's free cash flow and its adequacy ratio both fell sharply between 1989 and 1992, and free cash flow was negative in all 4 years. The adequacy ratio fell from 0.95 to 0.65. These developments suggest declining adequacy, but it is not clear that cash flows were inadequate in all 4 years. As discussed above, the measure of fixed assets spending used in these calculations includes both capital maintenance and spending to expand the company's productive capacity.

One way to gauge the amount of capital maintenance is to compare total fixed assets spending to depreciation and amortization:

(8) cash reinvestment ratio =

$$\frac{\text{depreciation and amortization + proceeds from fixed assets sales}}{\text{fixed assets spending}}$$

An increasing reinvestment ratio suggests a decreasing fraction of fixed assets spending devoted to expanding productive capacity. Depreciation is not an accurate measure of capital consumption, but it provides a useful gauge of a business's minimum reinvestment requirements. When substantial write-offs, rapid price inflation, or rapid technological change occurs, accrual-basis estimates of depreciation tend to understate the rate of capital consumption. As a case in point, the modest increase in International Paper's reinvestment ratio in 1992 excludes the effects of the write-offs that the company reported. Overall, the rising reinvestment ratio and the falling adequacy ratio tend to reinforce the impression of deteriorating financial strength suggested by the company's increasing reliance on outside financing.

A related measure of cash flow adequacy is the asset replacement ratio:

(9) asset replacement ratio =

$$\frac{\text{cash provided by operations - dividends}}{\text{average investment in assets}}$$

INTERNATIONAL PAPER COMPANY
Analysis of Cash Flow Adequacy

(in millions, except ratios for years ended December 31)

1989	1990	1991	1992	
$1,601	$1,440	$1,251	$1,205	Cash Provided by Operations + Inventory Additions
1,339	1,409	1,328	1,531	Less: Fixed assets spending
154	55	74	127	Inventory additions
187	183	186	206	Dividends
($ 79)	($ 207)	($ 337)	($ 659)	**Free Cash Flow** ·
$ 559	$ 667	$ 725	$ 850	Addendum: Depreciation and Amortization
0.95	0.87	0.79	0.65	Cash Flow Adequacy Ratio
0.42	0.47	0.55	0.56	Cash Reinvestment Ratio
0.12	0.10	0.08	0.06	Asset Replacement Ratio

80

The asset replacement ratio alters the ranking of cash uses presented in the calculation of free cash flow:

(10) cash provided by operations – dividends = free cash flow
                                                    + fixed assets spending

In this ratio, dividends and inventory additions come before purchases of fixed assets. The presumption is that all of the cash from operations that remains after dividends are paid will go toward the purchase of fixed assets. When free cash flow is negative, as in International Paper's case, that presumption is warranted.

This name of this ratio is misleading because the ratio does not measure actual asset replacement. Instead, it measures the adequacy of operating cash flows to fund fixed assets spending. According to one noted authority, operating cash flows should suffice to replace between 8 and 10 percent of the stock of assets annually.* The analysis of cash flow adequacy shows that International Paper fell short of this mark in 1992, which tends to confirm the downward trends of free cash flow and the adequacy ratio.

---

* Bernstein, Leopold A., *Financial Statement Analysis: Theory, Application, and Interpretation*, 4th ed. (Homewood, IL: Irwin, 1989), p. 567.

				As percentages of 1989 levels (index numbers or trend percentages)			Annual percent changes		
	Common-Size Analysis*								
1989	1990	1991	1992	1990	1991	1992	1990	1991	1992
1.00	1.00	1.00	1.00	90	78	75	−10.1	−13.1	−3.7
0.84	0.98	1.06	1.27	105	99	114	5.2	−5.7	15.3
0.10	0.04	0.06	0.11	36	48	82	−64.3	34.5	71.6
0.12	0.13	0.15	0.17	98	99	110	−2.1	1.6	10.8
(0.05)	(0.14)	(0.27)	(0.55)	262	427	834	162.0	62.8	95.5
0.35	0.46	0.58	0.71	119	130	152	19.3	8.7	17.2

cash flow adequacy ratio = $\dfrac{\text{cash provided by operations + inventory additions}}{\text{fixed assets spending + inventory additions + dividends}}$

cash reinvestment ratio = $\dfrac{\text{depreciation and amortization + proceeds from fixed assets sales}}{\text{fixed assets spending}}$

asset replacement ratio = $\dfrac{\text{cash provided by operations – dividends}}{\text{average investment in assets}}$

* Detail items may not add up to totals because of round-off error.

81

FURTHER READING

Related Works

Loth, Richard B., *How to Profit from Reading Annual Reports* (Chicago: Dearborn Financial Publishing, 1993).

Tracey, John A., *How to Read a Financial Report* (New York: John Wiley & Sons, 1980).

Woelfel, Charles J., *Financial Statement Analysis: The Investor's Self-Study Guide to Interpreting & Analyzing Financial Statements*, rev. ed. (Chicago: Probus Publishing, 1994).

AIER Publications

Larsen, Bruno M., "The A-Z Vocabulary for Investors," *Economic Education Bulletin* (November 1986, rev. June 1991), Vol. 26, No. 11.

Pratt, Lawrence S., "How to Invest Wisely," *Economic Education Bulletin* (January 1993), Vol. 33, No. 1.

Welker, Edward P., "How Safe is Your Bank?" *Economic Education Bulletin* (January 1992), Vol. 32, No. 1.
    This bulletin illustrates an application of ratio analysis.

Textbooks

Bernstein, Leopold A., *Financial Statement Analysis: Theory, Application, and Interpretation*, 4th ed. (Homewood, IL: Irwin, 1989).

Cottle, Sidney, Roger F. Murray, and Frank E. Block, *Graham and Dodd's Security Analysis*, 5th ed. (New York: McGraw-Hill, 1988).
    This is the classic text on investment analysis.

Meigs, Robert F., and Walter B. Meigs, *Accounting: The Basis for Business Decisions*, 8th ed. (New York: McGraw-Hill, 1990).
    There are many other introductory accounting texts on the market; they all say essentially the same thing.

White, Gerald I., and Ashwinpaul C. Sondhi, eds., *CFA Readings in Financial Statement Analysis*, 2nd. ed. (Charlottesville, VA: Association for Investment Management and Research, 1990).

Periodicals

AAII Journal (Chicago: American Association of Individual Investors, monthly).

Better Investing (Royal Oak, MI: National Association of Investors Corporation, monthly).

Financial Accounting Series (Norwalk, CT: Financial Accounting Standards Board, monthly).
    This series includes Statements of Financial Accounting Standards and Statements of Financial Accounting Concepts.

GLOSSARY

Acid-test ratio (also called *quick ratio*): the ratio of cash plus temporary investments plus receivables to total current liabilities.

Account receivable: a balance owed to a business by a customer as the result of sales of merchandise or services on credit.

Accounting period: the period covered by a set of financial statements, usually a quarter or a year.

Accrual: the recognition of a future cash receipt or payment. On the balance sheet, accruals denote liabilities for deferred payment of expenses.

Additional paid-in capital (also called *capital surplus* and *paid-in capital*): the cumulative proceeds of a corporation's offerings of stock at prices in excess of par value.

Adjusted operating cash flow: the sum of cash provided by operations, cash payments for income taxes, and cash payments for net interest.

Allocation: the process of systematically apportioning a cash outlay or receipt to the expenses or revenues of several accounting periods.

Allowance for doubtful accounts (also called *allowance*): a valuation account that contains an estimate of the portion of accounts receivable that is uncollectible.

Amortization: the process of allocating a revenue, expense, gain, or loss over several accounting periods by recording the transaction as an asset or liability as appropriate and then writing down the value of the asset or liability systematically in subsequent accounting periods, recognizing the amount of the write-down as an expense (in the case of an asset) or revenue (in the case of a liability).

Asset: a physical, technical, or financial resource owned by an enterprise. The FASB has defined assets as follows:

Assets are probable future economic benefits obtained or controlled by a particular entity as a result of past transactions or events.

An asset has three essential characteristics: (a) it embodies a probable future benefit that involves a capacity, singly or in combination with other assets, to contribute directly or indirectly to future net cash inflows, (b) a particular entity can obtain the benefit and control others' access to it, and (c) the transaction or other event giving rise to the entity's right to or control of the benefit has already occurred. Assets commonly have other features that help identify them — for example, assets may be acquired at a cost and they may be tangible, exchangeable, or legally enforceable. However, those features are

asset replacement ratio

not essential characteristics of assets. Their absence, by itself, is not sufficient to preclude an item's qualifying as an asset. That is, assets may be acquired without cost, they may be intangible, and although not exchangeable they may be usable by the entity in producing or distributing other goods or services. Similarly, although the ability of an entity to obtain benefit from an asset and to control others' access to it generally rests on a foundation of legal rights, legal enforceability of a claim to the benefit is not a prerequisite for a benefit to qualify as an asset if the entity has the ability to obtain and control the benefit in other ways.*

Asset replacement ratio: cash provided by operations less dividend payments, stated as a percentage of the average investment in assets. This ratio is a measure of the rate at which an enterprise can replace its stock of assets without relying on outside financing.

Audit: an examination of an enterprise's accounting records and procedures to determine whether the enterprise's financial statements conform to generally accepted accounting principles (GAAP). The auditors must be independent public accountants who proceed in accordance with generally accepted auditing standards.

Average cost method: a method of valuing the units remaining in an inventory at the end of an accounting period. Average cost is the total cost of purchases during the period plus the value of the beginning inventory divided by the sum of the number of units purchased and the number of units in the beginning inventory.

Balance sheet (also called *statement of financial condition, statement of condition, statement of financial position,* and *statement of assets and liabilities*): a financial statement that lists the values of the assets, liabilities, and equity or net assets of an enterprise on a particular date.

Bond: an interest-bearing long-term debt security.

Book value (also called *capital, equity,* and *net worth*): the difference between a business enterprise's total assets and its total liabilities. Book value is the residual interest that the owners of a business hold in the assets of the business after its liabilities have been settled.

Capital: this word is used in many different ways. In financial statements, it generally is synonymous with *book value, equity,* and *net worth.*

Capital lease (also called *financial lease*): a rental agreement that in-

---

* Financial Accounting Standards Board of the Financial Accounting Foundation, "Statement of Financial Accounting Concepts No. 6: Elements of Financial Statements," *Financial Accounting Series* 17 (December 1985), pp. 10-11.

cludes most of the features of outright ownership. A capital lease is an alternative to cash purchase and to borrowing as a means of financing the use of equipment.

Capital maintenance: investments made to maintain an enterprise's existing scale of operations. Depending on the context, capital maintenance can apply to both the physical and the financial size of an enterprise's capital stock.

Capital surplus (also called *additional paid-in capital* and *paid-in capital*): the cumulative proceeds of a corporation's offerings of stock at prices in excess of par value.

Capitalization ratio: long-term liabilities divided by the sum of long-term liabilities and total equity. There are a multitude of possible adjustments to this basic formula.

Carrying value: the balance of an account adjusted for a related valuation account.

Cash: currency and checking-account balances. In common usage, cash includes cash equivalents, which are highly liquid short-term debt securities such as Treasury bills and commercial paper.

Cash fixed charges coverage (see also *fixed charges ratio*): the ratio of adjusted operating cash flow to fixed charges. This ratio measures the margin by which an enterprise's operations cover interest payments and repayments of long-term debt.

Cash flow: a payment or receipt of cash.

Cash flow adequacy: the degree to which a business's cash flows from operations can fund fixed assets spending, inventory additions, and dividends, in that order. If cash flows are inadequate, the business will have to rely on outside financing to conduct some of these activities.

Cash flow adequacy ratio: the ratio of cash provided by operations plus inventory additions to fixed assets spending plus inventory additions plus dividend payments.

Cash flow from financing: a transaction involving both a cash receipt or payment and a change in equity or in long-term liabilities, including the current portion of long-term debt. Cash flows from financing exclude operating cash flows, which produce changes in retained earnings, an equity account.

Cash flow from investments: a transaction involving both a cash receipt or payment and a change in a noncurrent asset.

Cash flow from operations: a cash flow involving a change in a current operating asset or liability, a revenue, expense, gain, or loss, or both.

Cash flow per share: cash provided by operations divided by the weighted average number of common shares outstanding.

Cash operating margin: cash provided by operations as a percentage of net sales.

Cash reinvestment ratio: depreciation and amortization plus proceeds from sales of fixed assets as a percentage of fixed assets spending. This ratio is a measure of the portion of fixed assets spending devoted to capital maintenance.

Cash return on assets: the ratio of adjusted operating cash flow to the average investment in assets.

Clean opinion (also called *unqualified opinion*): a report of independent accountants affirming that an enterprise's financial statements are fairly presented in all material respects, and in accordance with GAAP.

Commitment: Commitments are agreements, usually formal contracts, to transact business in the future. Examples of commitments include purchase orders, long-term purchase and supply contracts, lines of credit, and employment contracts.

Common stock: the class of stock created when a business incorporates. Owners of common stock have the lowest-priority claim on a corporation's assets in a liquidation proceeding. A corporation may not pay dividends on common stock until it pays dividends on preferred stock, if any.

Comprehensive income: the sum of revenues, expenses, gains, and losses during an accounting period.

Consolidation: the process of combining the accounting records of an enterprise and its subsidiaries to produce a single set of financial statements. Consolidation involves adding together comparable account balances of a parent and its subsidiaries and then netting out the effects of transactions within the organization as a whole.

Contingent liability: Contingent liabilities are losses or obligations that may result from past events or transactions, pending some future outcome or decision. Examples of contingent liabilities include loan guarantees and pending litigation.

Contra-asset account: a valuation account used to adjust the carrying value of an asset.

Corporation: a business that raises funds by issuing shares certifying a proportional ownership stake in some or all of the business's equity.

Cost of goods sold (sometimes called *cost of products sold*): purchasing and production expenses attributable to the merchandise sold during an accounting period. Technically, the cost of goods sold should include depreciation of production equipment, although in practice such depreciation often is listed separately.

Cost principle: an accounting rule that requires enterprises to record acquisitions of assets at cost.

Cumulative effect of changes in accounting principles: when an enterprise changes the set of accounting principles that it uses, it must compute what the earnings of previous periods would have been under the new set of principles. The enterprise then must add the cumulative differences between reported earnings and recomputed earnings to earnings for the current period. This amount is the cumulative effect of changes in accounting principles.

Current: expected to be liquidated or settled within 1 year or the average duration of one operating cycle, whichever is longer.

Current ratio: current assets divided by current liabilities. This ratio was once a primary indicator of solvency.

Debt-equity ratio: total liabilities divided by total equity. There are a multitude of possible adjustments to this basic formula.

Debt ratio: total liabilities divided by total assets. There are a multitude of possible adjustments to this basic formula.

Debt refinancing ratio: the ratio of reduction of debt to issuance of debt. If this ratio is below 1, an enterprise is increasing its leverage. If the ratio is above 1, it is reducing its debt burden. The ratio measures an enterprise's reliance on debt as a source of financing.

Deferral: the process of recording cash flows during the current period as assets and liabilities to be recognized as expenses and revenues in future periods.

Deferred charges: costs that an enterprise incurs that it expects to benefit its operations in more than one accounting period. Examples include moving costs and reorganization costs. An enterprise amortizes a deferred charge over the expected duration of the effect of the transaction that incurred the charge.

Deferred income taxes: a liability that accrues as a business recognizes income or gains for financial reporting purposes but not for tax purposes. The business recognizes the taxes due later as a current expense. Some businesses also maintain deferred income-tax accounts on the asset side of the balance sheet. These accounts accumulate payments of tax due immediately on income or gains that a business defers for financial reporting purposes.

Deficit: in a corporation, negative retained earnings. In partnerships and sole proprietorships, which do not make a distinction between retained earnings and paid-in capital, a deficit is simply negative equity. Similarly, a deficit in a nonprofit enterprise denotes negative net assets.

Depletion: the amortization of the costs of acquiring natural resources.

Depreciation: the amortization of the costs of acquiring buildings, plant, equipment, and other fixed assets.

Dilution: the reduction in the interests of a corporation's existing stockholders due to the issuance of additional common stock at disadvantageous terms.

Direct method: the computation of net cash flows from operations by taking the net total of a list of operating cash inflows and outflows.

Discontinued operations: divisions, subsidiaries, or entire business lines that an enterprise has sold or liquidated or plans to sell or liquidate.

Discounting: (1) the sale of receivables to third parties before maturity, usually for less than face value; (2) reducing the value of a price or payment.

Dividend yield: the ratio of a corporation's dividend per share to its market price per share.

Earnings: at its broadest, the sum of revenues, expenses, gains, and losses for an accounting period. There are many different ways to measure earnings, depending on which items are included.

Earnings from operations (also called *income from operations* and *operating earnings*): revenues from an enterprise's principal activities (operating revenues) net of expenses attributable to those activities (operating expenses). This measure usually excludes the portion of the provision for income taxes attributable to the enterprise's principal activities.

Earnings multiple (also called *price-earnings ratio*, *P-E ratio*, *price-earnings multiple*, *multiple*, and *times earnings*): market price divided by earnings per common share before adjustment for extraordinary items. Estimated future per-share earnings often are used in this ratio.

Earnings per share (EPS): more accurately called earnings per *common* share, this is earnings less preferred dividend requirements all divided by the weighted average number of common shares outstanding during the accounting period. When a corporation's capital structure is such that current common shareholders risk more than a 3 percent dilution of their interests, the corporation must present *primary* and *fully diluted* EPS in its audited financial statements. These measures account for the potential dilution. Fully diluted EPS is the more conservative measure.

Economic entity: an organization that controls resources or incurs obligations, or both. Economic entities include for-profit enterprises (businesses), nonprofit enterprises, governments, and households.

Efficiency: the degree to which a business can minimize the cost of existing operations by maximizing the use of resources.

Enterprise: a business or a nonprofit organization.

Equity (also called *book value, capital,* and *net worth*): the difference between a business enterprise's total assets and its total liabilities. Equity is the residual interest that the owners of a business hold in the assets of the business after its liabilities have been settled.

Expense: strictly speaking, a cash outlay attributable to an enterprise's principal activities. The cash outlay need not occur in the same accounting period in which the expense is recognized. In common usage, many losses are labeled expenses and some expenses are labeled losses.

Extraordinary item: a gain or loss that is material, unusual, and not expected to recur in the foreseeable future. Extraordinary items often are disaster-related.

Extras: noncash distributions to a corporation's shareholders, including spin-offs, warrants, rights, and stock dividends.

Financial Accounting Standards Board (FASB): an independent rule-making organization for the accounting profession.

Financial lease (also called *capital lease*): a rental agreement that includes most of the features of outright ownership. A financial lease is an alternative to cash purchase and to borrowing as a means of financing the use of equipment.

Financial leverage index: the ratio of return on equity to return on assets. When it exceeds 1, this ratio indicates a business's effective use of leverage.

Financial statement: a summary report on the financial operating results of an enterprise (the changes in its accounts during a given period) or on its financial position (the end-of-period balances of its accounts).

First-in, first-out (FIFO) method: a method of valuing the units remaining in an inventory at the end of an accounting period. The unit prices

fixed charges ratio

of the most recent purchases are applied to units remaining in inventory.

Fixed charges ratio (see also *cash fixed charges coverage*): the ratio of pretax operating earnings to the sum of net interest expense and principal repayment requirements. This ratio is a conservative measure of long-term solvency.

Fixed assets: properties, plant, equipment, and natural resources.

Flexibility: the degree to which a business can minimize the cost of expanding its operations by keeping resources in reserve.

Foreign currency translation adjustment: the accumulation of discrepancies arising from the consolidation of the financial statements of foreign subsidiaries. The foreign currency translation adjustment appears in the equity or net assets section of the parent enterprise's balance sheet. The discrepancies arise because equity accounts are translated at different exchange rates than those used for asset and liability accounts.

Free cash flow: this phrase is used to describe many different quantities. In this book, it is the margin by which the sum of inventory additions and cash provided by operations exceeds fixed assets spending plus inventory additions plus dividends. The notion behind any formula for free cash flow is to determine the amount of cash that a business has at its discretion after covering certain important nonoperating items, such as fixed assets spending. Two important uses for this residual cash are repayment of debt and investments in affiliates.

Fund: a subset of accounts in the books of a nonprofit enterprise. A fund consists of assets and liabilities used for a specific purpose (*e.g.*, current operations, buildings, equipment, endowment, etc.) and the resulting net assets.

Fund balances: a synonym for the net assets of a nonprofit enterprise.

Funds statement (also called *statement of cash flows*, *statement of changes in financial position*, and *statement of sources and applications of funds*, or *source & app*): a financial statement that reconciles an enterprise's beginning and ending cash balances for a given accounting period by listing the various sources and uses of cash.

Gain: a cash receipt not attributable to an enterprise's principal activities and not a donation to or investment in the enterprise. The cash receipt need not occur in the same period in which the gain is recognized. In common usage, some gains are labeled revenues.

Generally Accepted Accounting Principles (GAAP): the set of rules that govern accounting practices in the United States.

Going-concern assumption: an accounting principle that requires accountants to value transactions on the assumption that an enterprise will continue to operate, unless there is specific evidence to the contrary. This assumption is a major justification for recording asset values at cost.

Goodwill: the excess of the purchase price of an acquisition over the fair market value of its net identifiable assets. Goodwill represents payment in recognition of the acquisition's above-average earnings potential.

Gross profit margin: gross profit on sales as a percentage of net sales.

Gross profit on sales: net sales less the cost of goods sold.

Horizontal analysis: the intertemporal comparison of the line items in an enterprise's financial statements and of key ratios computed from those statements.

Hurdle rate of return: the rate of return necessary to make an investment worthwhile. This rate usually equals the cost of financing the investment.

Identifiable assets: assets other than goodwill.

Income from operations (also called *earnings from operations* and *operating earnings*): revenues from an enterprise's principal activities (operating revenues) net of expenses attributable to those activities (operating expenses). This measure usually excludes the portion of the provision for income taxes attributable to the enterprise's principal activities.

Income statement (also called *P&L, results of operations, statement of earnings, statement of income, statement of operations,* and *statement of profit and loss*): a financial statement that lists an enterprise's revenues, expenses, gains, and losses for an accounting period and the total of those items. The total for a business enterprise is called earnings or net income, and the total for a nonprofit organization is called the change in net assets or the change in fund balances.

Indirect method: the computation of net cash flows from operations by adding noncash expenses and increases in current liabilities to net income, and subtracting noncash revenues and increases in current assets.

Interest coverage ratio (also called *times interest earned*): the ratio of pretax operating earnings to net interest expense. This ratio measures a business's long-term solvency.

Investment in assets: total assets plus accumulated depreciation less current operating liabilities (current liabilities except dividends payable, notes payable, and the current portion of long-term debt).

Last-in, first-out (LIFO) method: a method of valuing the units remaining in an inventory at the end of an accounting period. The unit prices of

leverage

the beginning inventory and the earliest purchases in the period are applied to units remaining in inventory.

Leverage: long-term borrowing. A lever is a device that allows the operator to move disproportionately large objects. Leverage allows equity owners to control a disproportionately large amount of assets.

Liability: a nonownership claim on a portion of the assets of an enterprise. The FASB has defined liabilities as follows:

Liabilities are probable future sacrifices of economic benefits arising from present obligations of a particular entity to transfer assets or provide services to other entities in the future as a result of past transactions or events.

A liability has three essential characteristics: (a) it embodies a present duty or responsibility to one or more other entities that entails settlement by probable future transfer or use of assets at a specified or determinable date, on occurrence of a specified event, or on demand, (b) the duty or responsibility obligates a particular entity, leaving it little or no discretion to avoid the future sacrifice, and (c) the transaction or other event obligating the entity has already happened. Liabilities commonly have other features that help identify them — for example, most liabilities require the obligated entity to pay cash to one or more identified other entities and are legally enforceable. However, those features are not essential characteristics of liabilities. Their absence, by itself, is not sufficient to preclude an item's qualifying as a liability. That is, liabilities may not require an entity to pay cash but to convey other assets, to provide or stand ready to provide services, or to use assets. And the identity of the recipient need not be known to the obligated entity before the time of settlement. Similarly, although most liabilities rest generally on a foundation of legal rights and duties, existence of a legally enforceable claim is not a prerequisite for an obligation to qualify as a liability if for other reasons the entity has the duty or responsibility to pay cash, to transfer other assets, or to provide services to another entity.*

Liquidate: to convert to cash.

Liquidity: the ease with which an asset can be converted to cash. By definition, cash is perfectly liquid. The amount of time that the conversion to cash takes is the most common measure of liquidity, although the cost of conversion often is a consideration.

Long-term: *noncurrent, i.e.,* not expected to be liquidated or settled

---

* Financial Accounting Standards Board of the Financial Accounting Foundation, "Statement of Financial Accounting Concepts No. 6: Elements of Financial Statements," *Financial Accounting Series* 17 (December 1985), p. 13.

within 1 year or one operating cycle, whichever is longer. This term is applied to liabilities much more often than to assets.

Loss: a cash payment not attributable to an enterprise's principal activities and not a payment to owners. The cash payment need not occur in the same period in which the loss is recognized. In common usage, many losses are labeled expenses and some expenses are labeled losses.

Lower of cost or market rule: an accounting rule that requires enterprises to carry assets at current market values when their market values fall below original cost.

Matching principle: a generally accepted accounting principle that requires enterprises to match the revenues generated during an accounting period with the expenses incurred to generate those revenues by recognizing expenses accordingly.

Material uncertainty: an unresolved matter that, when resolved, has some probability of making a significant impact on an enterprise's financial statements.

Minority interest: the share of the net assets of a majority-owned subsidiary that the parent enterprise does not own. Minority interest appears as a liability and as a deduction from earnings in the accounts of a parent enterprise.

Multiple (also called *price-earnings ratio, P-E ratio, price-earnings multiple, earnings multiple,* and *times earnings*): market price divided by earnings per common share before adjustment for extraordinary items. Estimated future per-share earnings often are used in this ratio.

Multiple-step income statement: an income statement that includes a computation of gross profit (step 1) followed by a computation of earnings (step 2).

Net assets: the difference between a nonprofit enterprise's total assets and its total liabilities. Net assets are the residual assets of a nonprofit that remain after its liabilities have been settled.

Net earnings (also called *net income*): revenues and gains for an accounting period net of expenses and losses.

Net identifiable assets: total assets less the sum of total liabilities and goodwill.

Net income: (also called *net earnings*): revenues and gains for an accounting period net of expenses and losses.

Net loss: negative net earnings.

net realizable value

Net realizable value: the market value of an asset less anticipated selling expenses.

Net sales: total sales revenues less allowances for discounts and returned merchandise.

Net worth: the difference between an enterprise's total assets and its total liabilities. In a business context, net worth is synonymous with *book value*, *capital*, and *equity*. In a nonprofit context, net worth is synonymous with *net assets*.

Noncurrent: not expected to be liquidated or settled within 1 year or one operating cycle, whichever is longer.

Note: a written promise to pay a debt. Notes often bear interest.

Off-balance-sheet financing: the use of sources of nonequity financing that do not appear as liabilities in an enterprise's accounts.

Operating cycle: in a manufacturing or merchandising company, the period comprising the production or purchase of goods, the sale of goods on account, and the conversion of accounts receivable to cash.

Operating earnings (also called *earnings from operations* and *income from operations*): revenues from an enterprise's principal activities (operating revenues) net of expenses attributable to those activities (operating expenses). This measure usually excludes the portion of the provision for income taxes attributable to the enterprise's principal activities.

Operating lease: a rental agreement that includes few of the features of outright ownership.

Operating profit margin (also called *operating margin*): pretax earnings from operations as a percentage of net sales.

Operating working capital: current operating assets (current assets except loans receivable from officers) less current operating liabilities (current liabilities except dividends payable, notes payable, and the current portion of long-term debt).

Other assets: a balance-sheet item that usually includes intangible assets such as copyrights, patents, trademarks and other intellectual property rights. Other assets sometimes includes deferred charges if they are not listed separately.

Overtrading: excessive turnover of an asset, which can restrict sales unnecessarily.

P&L (also called *income statement, results of operations, statement of earnings, statement of income, statement of operations*, and *statement of* *profit and loss*): a financial statement that lists an enterprise's revenues, expenses, gains, and losses for an accounting period and the total of those items. The total for a business enterprise is called earnings or net income, and the total for a nonprofit organization is called the change in net assets or the change in fund balances.

Paid-in capital (also called *capital surplus* and *additional paid-in capital*): the cumulative proceeds of a corporation's offerings of stock at prices in excess of par value.

Parent enterprise: an enterprise that owns the majority of the equity in a business.

Partnership: a form of business organization in which the ownership of the equity of a business is allocated by an agreement among the principals in the business, who are called partners.

Par value (also called *stated value*): the legal minimum book value of a class of a corporation's stock. A corporation's directors cannot declare a dividend that would reduce the total book value of equity below the total par value of the corporation's stock. Some states do not require a corporation to establish a par value for its stock.

Payable: a liability for the amount of a credit account, a note, or an accrued expense.

Preferred stock: classes of stock that take priority over common stock in liquidation proceedings. Preferred stock also may be preferred as to dividends, if a corporation cannot pay a dividend on common stock when in arrears on its preferred dividends.

Present value: the sum of a series of future cash payments, *e.g.*, dividends, interest, or principal, adjusted for the time value of money. The time-value adjustment involves discounting future payments by the amount of interest foregone by not receiving them immediately.

Pretax earnings: earnings from operations (before income taxes) less net interest expense and certain other nonoperating items.

Price-earnings ratio (also called *P-E ratio, price-earnings multiple, earnings multiple, multiple*, and *times earnings*): market price divided by earnings per common share before adjustment for extraordinary items. Estimated future per-share earnings often are used in this ratio.

Profitability: the extent to which a business's revenues exceed its expenses. Profitability usually is measured as a percentage of revenues, assets, or equity.

Provision for income taxes: the income tax expense for the current

quality

accounting period plus the net addition to deferred income tax liabilities.

Quality: the likelihood of an asset's conversion to cash without any loss.

Quality of earnings: the ratio of operating cash flows to net earnings.

Quick assets: the sum of cash, temporary investments, and receivables.

Quick ratio (also called *acid-test ratio*): the ratio of cash plus temporary investments plus receivables to total current liabilities.

Ratio analysis: the comparison of line items and groups of items within a set of financial statements. Ratios are particularly useful for comparing the financial statements of two or more enterprises.

Realization principle: a generally accepted accounting principle that requires enterprises to recognize revenues in the accounting period in which they sell goods or render services, regardless of the timing of cash receipts.

Receivable: a credit account or a note from the lender's point of view; the lender holds the right to receive the proceeds when the account or note is liquidated. *Receivables* usually refers to the sum of accounts receivable and notes receivable.

Recourse: a common provision of discounting transactions that requires sellers of receivables to continue to assume the risk of delinquent and uncollectible accounts.

Report of independent accountants (also called *report of independent auditors*): the auditors' opinion of the fairness of presentation of a set of audited financial statements.

Results of operations (also called *income statement, P&L, statement of earnings, statement of income, statement of operations,* and *statement of profit and loss*): a financial statement that lists an enterprise's revenues, expenses, gains, and losses for an accounting period and the total of those items. The total for a business enterprise is called earnings or net income, and the total for a nonprofit organization is called the change in net assets or the change in fund balances.

Retained earnings (also called *reinvested earnings* and *profit employed in the business*): the cumulative sum of additions to a corporation's equity, consisting of earnings net of dividends.

Return on assets: the ratio of pretax operating earnings to average total assets. This ratio measures the efficiency of a business's operations and it is a popular measure of return on investment.

Return on equity: the ratio of earnings applicable to common shareholders to average common shareholders' equity. This ratio is a popular measure of return on investment.

Return on investment: a business's earnings as a percentage of the resource base used to produce those earnings.

Revenue: strictly speaking, a cash receipt attributable to an enterprise's principal activities. The cash receipt need not occur in the same accounting period in which the revenue is recognized. In common usage, many gains are labeled revenues.

Single-step income statement: an income statement that presents a computation of earnings without a computation of gross profit.

Sole proprietorship: a form of business organization in which one principal, the sole proprietor, owns all of the equity of a business.

Solvency: an enterprise's ability to meet its obligations promptly.

Source & app (also called *funds statement*, *statement of cash flows*, *statement of changes in financial position*, and *statement of sources and applications of funds*): a financial statement that reconciles an enterprise's beginning and ending cash balances for a given accounting period by listing the various sources and uses of cash.

Specific identification method: a method of valuing the units remaining in an inventory at the end of an accounting period. The method is to add up the prices paid for each unit remaining in inventory.

Stated value (also called *par value*): the legal minimum book value of a class of a corporation's stock. A corporation's directors cannot declare a dividend that would reduce the total book value of equity below the total stated value of the corporation's stock. Some states do not require a corporation to establish a stated value for its stock.

Statement of assets and liabilities (also called *balance sheet*, *statement of financial condition*, *statement of condition*, *statement of financial position*): a financial statement that lists the values of the assets, liabilities, and capital of an enterprise on a particular date.

Statement of cash flows (also called *funds statement*, *statement of changes in financial position*, and *statement of sources and applications of funds*, or *source & app*): a financial statement that reconciles an enterprise's beginning and ending cash balances for a given accounting period by listing the various sources and uses of cash.

Statement of changes in net assets (also called *statement of changes in fund balances*): a financial statement that reconciles the beginning-of-period and end-of-period net assets of a nonprofit enterprise by accounting

statement of condition

for net earnings and donations for the period. In many cases, this statement also documents transfers among an enterprise's various funds.

Statement of condition (also called *balance sheet, statement of financial condition, statement of financial position, statement of assets and liabilities*): a financial statement that lists the values of the assets, liabilities, and equity or net assets of an enterprise on a particular date.

Statement of earnings (also called *income statement, P&L, results of operations, statement of income, statement of operations,* and *statement of profit and loss*): a financial statement that lists an enterprise's revenues, expenses, gains, and losses for an accounting period and the total of those items. The total for a business enterprise is called earnings or net income, and the total for a nonprofit organization is called the change in net assets or the change in fund balances.

Statement of financial condition (also called *balance sheet, statement of condition, statement of financial position, statement of assets and liabilities*): a financial statement that lists the values of the assets, liabilities, and equity or net assets of an enterprise on a particular date.

Statement of income / operations (also called *income statement, P&L, results of operations, statement of earnings, statement of operations,* and *statement of profit and loss*): a financial statement that lists an enterprise's revenues, expenses, gains, and losses for an accounting period and the total of those items. The total for a business enterprise is called earnings or net income, and the total for a nonprofit organization is called the change in net assets or the change in fund balances.

Statement of owners' equity (also called *statement of partners' equity* and *statement of shareholders' equity*): a financial statement that reconciles a business's beginning-of-period and end-of-period total equity by accounting for the disposition of earnings, investments by owners, and distributions to owners during an accounting period.

Statement of profit and loss (also called *income statement, P&L, results of operations, statement of earnings, statement of income,* and *statement of operations*): a financial statement that lists an enterprise's revenues, expenses, gains, and losses for an accounting period and the total of those items. The total for a business enterprise is called earnings or net income, and the total for a nonprofit organization is called the change in net assets or the change in fund balances.

Statement of retained earnings: a financial statement that accounts for a corporation's allocation of net earnings between dividends and the retained earnings account.

Statement of shareholders'/ share-owners'/ stockholders' equity (also called *statement of owners' equity* and *statement of partners' equity*): a financial statement that reconciles a business's beginning-of-period and end-of-period total equity by accounting for the disposition of earnings, investments by owners, and distributions to owners during an accounting period.

Statement of sources and applications of funds (also called *funds statement, statement of cash flows, statement of changes in financial position*, and *source & app*): a financial statement that reconciles an enterprise's beginning and ending cash balances for a given accounting period by listing the various sources and uses of cash.

Subsidiary: a business in which one enterprise controls the election of the board of directors, usually by owning the majority of that business's equity.

Surplus: a synonym for net assets, often used in the financial statements of nonprofit enterprises.

Tax allocation: an accounting practice businesses use to reconcile tax expenses recognized in published financial statements with actual tax payments. Tax allocation is necessary because of the many differences between income as defined in tax statutes and income as measured by applying generally accepted accounting principles (GAAP). Businesses reconcile statutory taxes with GAAP taxes by using deferred income tax liabilities and assets to allocate tax payments among the expenses of several accounting periods.

Times earnings (also called *price-earnings ratio, P-E ratio, price-earnings multiple, earnings multiple*, and *multiple*): market price divided by earnings per common share before adjustment for extraordinary items. Estimated future per-share earnings often are used in this ratio.

Times interest earned (also called *interest coverage ratio*): the ratio of pretax operating earnings to net interest expense. This ratio measures a business's long-term solvency.

Total return: the sum of a corporation's dividends, extras, and the change in its share price for a given period, usually expressed as a percentage of the beginning share price.

Treasury stock: stock that a corporation has issued and subsequently repurchased.

Turnover: the ratio of net sales volume to the value of a balance-sheet item.

Unqualified opinion (also called *clean opinion*): a report of independent

valuation account

accountants affirming that an enterprise's financial statements are fairly presented in all material respects, and in accordance with GAAP.

Valuation account: an account used to adjust for changing circumstances the amount initially recorded in an asset, liability, or equity account. A valuation account is part of the related account and is neither an asset nor a liability in its own right. The valuation accounts that appear in financial statements typically are contra-asset accounts, such as depreciation and allowances.

Vertical analysis: the comparison of the size of each line item in a financial statement to some benchmark item on that statement. Sales and total assets are the most common benchmark items.

Working capital (see also *operating working capital*): current assets minus current liabilities.

PUBLICATIONS
AND SUSTAINING MEMBERSHIPS

You can receive our twice monthly *Research Reports* and monthly *Economic Education Bulletin* by entering a **Sustaining Membership** for only $16 quarterly or $59 annually. If you wish to receive only the *Economic Education Bulletin*, you may enter an **Education Membership** for $25 annually.

INVESTMENT GUIDE

At your request, AIER will forward your payment for a subscription to the *Investment Guide* published by American Investment Services, Inc. (AIS). The *Guide* is issued once a month at a price of $49 per year (add $13 for foreign airmail). It provides guidance to investors, both working and retired, of modest and large means, to help them preserve the real value of their wealth during these difficult financial times. AIS is wholly owned by AIER and is the only investment advisory endorsed by AIER.